CASCADIA
GARDENING
SERIES

Water-Wise Vegetables

For the Maritime Northwest Gardener

Steve Solomon

Sasquatch Books
Seattle

Printed in the United States of America

Cover design: Kris Morgan Design
Cover photograph: Cliff Fiess Photography
Interior design: Lynne Faulk Design
Interior illustration: Celeste Henriquez
Interior photographs: Greg Lawler/Small Planet Photography
Composition: Scribe Typography

Library of Congress Cataloging in Publication Data
Solomon, Steve.
    Water-wise vegetables / Steve Solomon.
        p. cm. — (Cascadia gardening series)
    Includes bibliographical references (p.) and index.
    ISBN 0-912365-75-7 : $8.95
    1. Vegetable gardening — Water conservation — Northwest Coast of
North America. I. Title. II. Series.
    SB321.S644 1993
    635'.0486'09795 — dc20   92-42242
                                                                  CIP

Published by Sasquatch Books
1931 Second Avenue
Seattle, Washington 98101
(206) 441-6202

Other titles in the Cascadia Gardening Series:
North Coast Roses, by Rhonda Massingham Hart
Winter Ornamentals, by Daniel Hinkley (forthcoming)
The Herb-Gardener's Handbook, by Mary Preus (forthcoming)

Contents

Gardening in the Maritime Northwest

The maritime Northwest—lying west of the Cascade Range and running from British Columbia to northern California—is often called Cascadia. With its warm dry summers and cool rainy winters, this region offers particular challenges to regional gardeners. In addition to its temperate but often unpredictable weather, Cascadia is characterized by glacial soils, dramatic topography, and a growing population that is straining water supplies in urban areas. It is also a land blessed with both a full spectrum of native flora and ideal growing conditions for a vast array of non-native plants.

The Cascadia Gardening Series addresses the challenges and benefits of gardening in the maritime Northwest. Topics in the series cover both ornamental and food crops, and provide experienced as well as novice gardeners with up-to-date information and advice. The series authors rely on local knowledge, personal experience, and the counsel of regional gardening experts. Cultivation data is adapted to regional microclimates and soils, and recommendations for maintaining a healthy garden are tailored to specific conditions. Each book includes suggestions for drought- and pest-resistance varieties, landscaping, irrigation techniques, and plant selection.

The goal of the series is to help gardeners increase their knowledge, understanding, and enjoyment of gardening in the maritime Northwest. Please let us know what you think of this book, and what topics you would like to see explored in upcoming books in the Cascadia Gardening Series.

Cascadia Gardening Series
Sasquatch Books
1931 Second Avenue
Seattle, WA 98101

—*The Editors*

Starting a New
Gardening Era

First, you should know why a maritime Northwest raised-bed gardener named Steve Solomon became worried about his dependence on irrigation.

I'm from Michigan. I moved to Lorane, Oregon, in April 1978 and homesteaded on 5 acres in what I thought at the time was a cool, showery green valley of liquid sunshine and rainbows. I intended to put in a big garden and grow as much of my own food as possible.

Two months later, in June, just as my garden began needing water, my so-called 15-gallon-per-minute well began to falter, yielding less and less with each passing week. By August it delivered about 3 gallons per minute. Fortunately, I wasn't faced with a completely dry well or one that had shrunk to below 1 gallon per minute, as I soon discovered many of my neighbors were cursed with. Three gallons per minute won't supply a fan nozzle or even a common impulse sprinkler, but I could still sustain my big raised-bed garden by watering all night, five or six nights a week, with a single, 2½-gallon-per-minute sprinkler that I moved from place to place.

I had repeatedly read that gardening in raised beds was the most productive vegetable growing method, required the least work, and was the most water-efficient system known. So, without adequate irrigation, I would have concluded that food self-sufficiency on my homestead was not possible. In late September of my first hot, rainless maritime Northwest summer, I could still run that single sprinkler. What a relief not to have invested every last cent in land that couldn't feed us.

For many succeeding years at Lorane, I raised lots of organically grown food on densely planted raised beds, but the realities of being a country gardener continued to remind me of how tenuous my irrigation supply actually was. We country folks have to be self-reliant: I am my own sanitation department, I maintain my own 800-foot-long driveway, the septic system puts me in the sewage business. A long, long response time to my 911 call means I'm my own self-defense force. And I'm my own water department.

Without regular and heavy watering during high summer, dense stands of vegetables become stunted in a matter of days. Pump failure has brought my raised-bed garden close to that several times. Before my frantic efforts got the water flowing again, I could feel the stressed-out garden screaming like a hungry baby.

As I came to understand our climate, I began to wonder about *complete* food self-sufficiency. How did the early pioneers irrigate their vegetables? There probably aren't more than a thousand homestead sites in the entire maritime Northwest with gravity water. Hand pumping into hand-carried buckets is impractical and extremely tedious. Wind-powered pumps are expensive and have severe limits.

The combination of dependably rainless summers, the realities of self-sufficient living, and my homestead's poor well turned out to be an opportunity. For I continued wondering about gardens and water, and discovered a method for growing a lush, productive vegetable garden on deep soil with little or no irrigation, in a climate that reliably provides 8 to 12 hot and virtually dry weeks every summer.

GARDENING WITH LESS IRRIGATION

Being a garden writer, I was on the receiving end of quite a bit of local lore. I had heard of someone growing unirrigated carrots on sandy soil in southern Oregon by sowing early and spacing the roots 1 foot apart in rows 4 feet apart. The carrots were reputed to grow to enormous sizes, and the overall yield in pounds per square foot occupied by the crop was not as low as one might think. I read that Native Americans in the Southwest grew remarkable desert gardens with little or no water. And that Native South Americans in the highlands of Peru and Bolivia grow food crops in a land with 8 to 12 inches of rainfall. So I had to wonder what our own pioneers did.

In 1987, we moved 50 miles south, to a much better homestead with more acreage and an abundant well. Ironically, only then did I grow my first summertime vegetable without irrigation. Being a low-key survivalist at heart, I was working at growing my own seeds. The main danger to attaining good germination is in repeatedly moistening developing seed. So, in early March 1988, I moved six winter-surviving savoy cabbage plants far beyond the irrigated soil of my raised-bed vegetable garden. I transplanted them 4 feet apart because blooming brassicas make huge sprays of flower stalks. I did not plan to water these plants at all, since cabbage seed forms during May and dries down during June as the soil naturally dries out.

That is just what happened. Except that one plant did something a little unusual, though not unheard of. Instead of completely going into bloom and then dying after setting a massive load of seed, this plant also threw a vegetative bud that grew a whole new cabbage among the seed stalks.

With increasing excitement I watched this head grow steadily larger through the hottest and driest summer I had ever experienced. Realizing I was witnessing Revelation, I gave the plant absolutely no water, though I did hoe out the weeds around it after I cut the seed stalks. I harvested the unexpected lesson at the end of September. The cabbage weighed 6 or 7 pounds and was sweet and tender.

Up to that time, all my gardening had been on thoroughly and uniformly watered raised beds. Now I saw that elbow room might be the key to gardening with little or no irrigation, so I began looking for more information about dry gardening and soil/water physics. In spring 1989, I tilled four widely separated, unirrigated experimental rows in which I tested an assortment of vegetable species spaced far apart in each row. Out of curiosity I decided to use absolutely no water, not even for sprinkling the seeds to get them germinating.

I sowed a bit of kale, savoy cabbage, Purple Sprouting broccoli, carrots, beets, parsnips, parsley, endive, dry beans, potatoes, French sorrel, and a couple of field cornstalks. I also tested one compact bush (determinate) and one sprawling (indeterminate) tomato plant. Many of these vegetables grew surprisingly well. I ate unwatered tomatoes July through September; kale, cabbages, parsley, and root crops fed us during the winter. The Purple Sprouting broccoli bloomed abundantly the next March.

In terms of quality, all the harvest was acceptable. The root vegetables were far larger but only a little bit tougher and quite a bit sweeter than usual. The potatoes yielded less than I'd been used to and had thicker than usual skin, but also had a better flavor and kept well through the winter.

The following year I grew two parallel gardens. One, my "insurance garden," was thoroughly irrigated, guaranteeing we would have plenty to eat. Another experimental garden of equal size was entirely unirrigated. There I tested larger plots of species that I hoped could grow through a rainless summer.

By July, growth on some species had slowed to a crawl and they looked a little gnarly. Wondering if a hidden cause of what appeared to be lack of moisture might actually be nutrient deficiencies, I tried spraying liquid fertilizer directly on these gnarly leaves, a practice called foliar feeding. It helped greatly because, I reasoned, most fertility is located in the topsoil, and when it gets dry the plants draw on subsoil moisture, so surface nutrients, though still present in the dry soil, become unobtainable. That being so, I reasoned that some of these species might do even better if they had just a little fertilized water. So I improvised a simple drip system and metered out 4 or 5 gallons of liquid fertilizer to some of the plants in late July and 4 gallons more in August. To some species, extra fertilized water (what I call "fertigation") hardly made any difference at all. But unirrigated winter squash vines, which were small and scraggly and yielded about 15 pounds of food, grew more lushly when given a few 5-gallon, fertilizer-fortified assists and yielded 50 pounds. Thirty-five pounds of squash for 25 extra gallons of water and a bit of extra nutrition is a pretty good exchange in my book.

The next year I integrated all this new information into just one garden. Water-loving species like lettuce and celery were grown through the summer on a large, thoroughly irrigated raised bed. The rest of the garden was given no irrigation at all or minimally metered-out fertigations. Some unirrigated crops were foliar fed weekly.

Everything worked in 1991! And I found still other species that I could grow surprisingly well on surprisingly small amounts of water—or none at all. So, the next year, 1992, I set up a sprinkler system to water the intensive raised bed and used the overspray to support species that grew better with some moisture supplementation; I continued using my improvised drip system to help still others, while keeping a large section of the garden entirely unwatered. And at the end of that summer I wrote this book.

What follows is not mere theory, not something I read about or saw others do. These techniques are tested and workable. The next-to-last chapter of this book contains a complete plan of my 1992 garden, with explanations and discussion of the reasoning behind it.

In *Water-Wise Vegetables* I assume that my readers already are growing food (probably on raised beds), already know how to adjust their gardening to this region's climate, and know how to garden with irrigation. If you don't have this background I suggest you read my other garden book, *Growing Vegetables West of the Cascades* (Sasquatch Books, 1989).

—*Steve Solomon*

Rainless Summers

CHAPTER 1

In the eastern United States, summertime rainfall can support gardens without irrigation but is just irregular enough to be worrisome. West of the Cascades we go into the summer growing season certain we must water regularly.

My own many-times-revised book *Growing Vegetables West of the Cascades* correctly emphasized that moisture-starved vegetables suffer greatly. Because I had not yet noticed how plant spacing affects soil moisture loss, in that book I stated a half-truth as law: Soil moisture loss averages 1½ inches per week during summer.

This loss estimate is generally true for raised-bed gardens west of the Cascades, so I recommended adding 1½ inches of water each week and even more during really hot weather.

Summertime Rainfall West of the Cascades (*in inches*)

Location	April	May	June	July	Aug.	Sep.	Oct.
Eureka, Calif.	3.0	2.1	0.7	0.1	0.3	0.7	3.2
Medford, Ore.	1.0	1.4	0.98	0.3	0.3	0.6	2.1
Eugene, Ore.	2.3	2.1	1.3	0.3	0.6	1.3	4.0
Portland, Ore.	2.2	2.1	1.6	0.5	0.8	1.6	3.6
Astoria, Ore.	4.6	2.7	2.5	1.0	1.5	2.8	6.8
Olympia, Wash.	3.1	1.9	1.6	0.7	1.2	2.1	5.3
Seattle, Wash.	2.4	1.7	1.6	0.8	1.0	2.1	4.0
Bellingham, Wash.	2.3	1.8	1.9	1.0	1.1	2.0	3.7
Vancouver, B.C.	3.3	2.8	2.5	1.2	1.7	3.6	5.8
Victoria, B.C.	1.2	1.0	0.9	0.4	0.6	1.5	2.8

Source: van der Leeden et al., *The Water Encyclopedia*, 2nd ed. (Chelsea, Mich.: Lewis Publishers, 1990).

Defined scientifically, drought is not lack of rain. It is a *dry soil condition* in which plant growth slows or stops and plant survival may be threatened. The earth loses water when wind blows, when sun shines, when air temperature is high, and when humidity is low. Of all these factors, air temperature most affects soil moisture loss.

Daily Maximum Temperature (°F) July/August Average

Eureka, Calif.	61
Medford, Ore.	89
Eugene, Ore.	82
Portland, Ore.	80
Astoria, Ore.	68
Olympia, Wash.	78
Seattle, Wash.	75
Bellingham, Wash.	74
Vancouver, B.C.	73
Victoria, B.C.	68

Source: *The Water Encyclopedia.*

The kind of vegetation growing on a particular plot as well as its density have even more to do with soil moisture loss than temperature or humidity or wind speed. And, surprising as it might seem, bare soil may not lose much moisture at all. I now know it is next to impossible to anticipate moisture loss from soil without first specifying the vegetation there. Evaporation from a large body of water, however, is mainly determined by weather, so reservoir evaporation measurements serve as a rough gauge of anticipated soil moisture loss.

Evaporation from Reservoirs *(inches per month)*

Location	April	May	June	July	Aug.	Sep.	Oct.
Seattle, Wash.	2.1	2.7	3.4	3.9	3.4	2.6	1.6
Baker, Ore.	2.5	3.4	4.4	6.9	7.3	4.9	2.9
Sacramento, Calif.	3.6	5.0	7.1	8.9	8.6	7.1	4.8

Source: *The Water Encyclopedia.*

From May through September during a normal year, a reservoir near Seattle loses about 16 inches of water by evaporation. The next chart shows how much water farmers expect to use to support conventional agriculture in various parts of the West. Comparing this data for Seattle with the estimates based on reservoir evaporation shows pretty good agreement. I include data for Umatilla and Yakima to show that much larger quantities of irrigation water are needed in really hot, arid places like Baker or Sacramento.

Estimated Irrigation Requirements During Growing Season (*in inches*)

Location	Duration	Amount
Umatilla/Yakima Valley	April–October	30
Willamette Valley	May–September	16
Puget Sound	May–September	14
Upper Rogue/Upper Umpqua Valley	March–September	18
Lower Rogue/Lower Coquille Valley	May–September	11
NW California	April–October	17

Source: *The Water Encyclopedia.*

In our region, gardens lose far more water than they get from rainfall during the summer growing season. At first glance, it seems impossible to garden without irrigation west of the Cascades. But there is water already present in the soil when the gardening season begins. By creatively using and conserving this moisture, some fortunate maritime Northwest gardeners can go through an entire summer without irrigating very much, and with some crops, irrigating not at all. Other gardeners, with less than ideal soil conditions, can still greatly reduce their dependence on irrigation.

Water-Wise
Science

CHAPTER 2

PLANTS ARE WATER

Like all other carbon-based life forms on earth, plants conduct their chemical processes in a water solution. Every substance that plants transport is dissolved in water. When insoluble starches and oils are required for plant energy, enzymes change them back into water-soluble sugars for movement to other locations. Even cellulose and lignin, insoluble structural materials that plants cannot convert back into soluble materials, are made from molecules that once were in solution.

Water is so essential that when a plant can no longer absorb as much water as it is losing, it wilts in self-defense. The drooping leaves transpire (evaporate) less moisture because the sun glances off them. Some weeds can wilt temporarily and resume vigorous growth as soon as their water balance is restored. But most vegetable species aren't as tough—moisture-stressed vegetables may survive, but once stressed, the quality of their yield usually drops markedly.

Yet in deep, open soil west of the Cascades, most vegetable species may be grown quite successfully with very little or no supplementary irrigation and without mulching, because they're capable of being supplied entirely by water already stored in the soil.

SOIL'S WATER-HOLDING CAPACITY

Soil is capable of holding on to quite a bit of water, mostly by adhesion. For example, I'm sure that at one time or another you have picked up a wet stone from a river or by the sea. A thin film of water clings to its surface. This is adhesion. The more surface area there is, the greater the amount of moisture that can be held by adhesion. If we crushed that stone into dust, we would greatly increase the amount of water that could adhere to the original material. Clay particles, it should be noted,

17

are so small that clay's ability to hold water is not as great as its mathematically computed surface area would indicate.

Surface Area of One Gram of Soil Particles

Particle type	Diameter in millimeters	Number per gram	Surface area in sq. cm.
Very coarse sand	2.00–1.00	90	11
Coarse sand	1.00–0.50	720	23
Medium sand	0.50–0.25	5,700	45
Fine sand	0.25–0.10	46,000	91
Very fine sand	0.10–0.05	772,000	227
Silt	0.05–0.002	5,776,000	454
Clay	Below 0.002	90,260,853,000	8,000,000

Source: Foth, Henry D., *Fundamentals of Soil Science*, 8th ed. (New York: John Wylie & Sons, 1990).

Comprehending this direct relationship between particle size, surface area, and water-holding capacity is so essential to understanding plant growth that the surface areas presented by various sizes of soil particles have been calculated. Soils are not composed of a single size of particle. If the mix is primarily sand, we call it a sandy soil. If the mix is primarily clay, we call it a clay soil. If the soil is a relatively equal mix of all three, containing no more than 35 percent clay, we call it a loam.

Available Moisture (*inches of water per foot of soil*)

Soil texture	Average amount
Very coarse sand	0.5
Coarse sand	0.7
Sandy	1.0
Sandy loam	1.4
Loam	2.0
Clay loam	2.3
Silty clay	2.5
Clay	2.7

Source: *Fundamentals of Soil Science*.

Adhering water films can vary greatly in thickness. But if the water molecules adhering to a soil particle become too thick, the force of adhesion becomes too weak to resist the force of gravity, and some water flows deeper into the soil. When water films are relatively thick, the soil feels wet and plant roots can easily absorb moisture. "Field capacity" is the term describing soil particles holding all the water they can against the force of gravity.

At the other extreme, the thinner the water films become, the more tightly they adhere and the drier the earth feels. At some degree of desiccation, roots are no longer forceful enough to draw on soil moisture as fast as the plants are transpiring. This condition is called the "wilting point." The term "available moisture" refers to the difference between field capacity and the amount of moisture left after the plants have died.

Clayey soil can provide plants with three times as much available water as sand, six times as much as a very coarse sandy soil. It might seem logical to conclude that a clayey garden would be the most drought resistant. But there's more to it. For some crops, deep sandy loams can provide just about as much usable moisture as clays. Sandy soils usually allow more extensive root development, so a plant with a naturally aggressive and deep root system may be able to occupy a much larger volume of sandy loam, ultimately coming up with more moisture than it could obtain from a heavy, airless clay. And sandy loams often have a clayey, moisture-rich subsoil.

Because of this interplay of factors, how much available water your own garden soil can provide and how much it will need to be supplemented with irrigation can be discovered only by trial.

How Soil Loses Water

Suppose we tilled a plot about April 1 and then measured soil moisture loss until October. Because plants growing around the edge might extend roots into our test plot and extract moisture, we'll make our tilled area 50 feet by 50 feet and make all our measurements in the center. And let's locate this imaginary plot in full sun on flat, uniform soil. And let's plant absolutely nothing in this bare earth. And all season let's rigorously hoe out every weed while it is still very tiny.

Let's also suppose it's been a typical maritime Northwest rainy winter, so on April 1 the soil is at field capacity, holding all the moisture it can. From early April until well into September the hot sun will beat down on this bare plot. Our summer rains generally come in insignificant installments and do not penetrate deeply; all of the rain quickly evaporates from the surface few inches without recharging deeper layers. Most readers would reason that a soil moisture measurement taken 6 inches down on September 1 should show very little water left. One foot down seems like it should be just as dry, and in fact, most gardeners would expect that there would be very little water found in the soil until we got down quite a few feet—if there were several feet of soil.

But that is not what happens! The hot sun does dry out the surface inches, but if we dig down 6 inches or so there will be almost as much water present in September as there was in April. Bare earth does not lose much water at all. Once a thin surface layer is completely desiccated, be it loose or compacted, virtually no further loss of moisture can occur.

The only soils that continue to dry out when bare are certain kinds of very heavy clays that form deep cracks. These ever-deepening openings allow atmospheric air to freely evaporate additional moisture. But if the cracks are filled with dust by surface cultivation, even this soil type ceases to lose water.

Soil functions as our bank account, holding available water in storage. In our climate soil is inevitably charged to capacity by winter rains, and then all summer growing plants make heavy withdrawals. But hot sun and wind working directly on soil don't remove much water; that is caused by hot sun and wind working on plant leaves, making them transpire moisture drawn from the earth through their root systems. Plants desiccate soil to the ultimate depth and lateral extent of their rooting ability, and then some. The size of vegetable root systems is greater than most gardeners would think. The amount of moisture potentially available to sustain vegetable growth is also greater than most gardeners think.

Rain and irrigation are not the only ways to replace soil moisture. If the soil body is deep, water will gradually come up from below the root zone by capillarity. Capillarity works by the very same force of adhesion that makes moisture stick to a soil particle. A column of water in a vertical tube (like a thin straw) adheres to the tube's inner surfaces. This adhesion tends to lift the edges of the column of water. As the tube's diameter becomes smaller the amount of lift becomes greater. Soil particles form interconnected pores that allow an inefficient capillary flow, recharging dry soil above. However, the drier soil becomes, the less effective capillary flow becomes. That is why a thoroughly desiccated surface layer only a few inches thick acts as a powerful mulch.

Industrial farming and modern gardening tend to discount the replacement of surface moisture by capillarity, considering this flow an insignificant factor compared with the moisture needs of crops. But conventional agriculture focuses on maximized yields through high plant densities. Capillarity *is* too slow to support dense crop stands where numerous root systems are competing, but when a single plant can, without any competition, occupy a large enough area, moisture replacement by capillarity becomes significant.

How Plants Obtain Water

Most gardeners know that plants acquire water and minerals through their root systems, and leave it at that. But the process is not quite that simple. The actively growing, tender root tips and almost microscopic root hairs close to the tip absorb most of the plant's moisture as they occupy new territory. As the root continues to extend, parts behind the tip cease to be effective because, as soil particles in direct contact with these tips and hairs dry out, the older roots thicken and develop a bark, while most of the absorbent hairs slough off. This rotation from being actively foraging tissue to becoming more passive conductive and supportive tissue is probably a survival adaptation, because the slow capillary movement of soil moisture fails to replace what the plant used as fast as the plant might like. The plant is far better off to aggressively seek new water in unoccupied soil than to wait for the soil its roots already occupy to be recharged.

A simple bit of old research magnificently illustrated the significance of this. A scientist named Dittmer observed in 1937 that a single potted ryegrass plant allocated only 1 cubic foot of soil to grow in made about 3 miles of new roots and root hairs every day. (Ryegrasses are known to make more roots than most plants.) I calculate that a cubic foot of silty soil offers about 30,000 square feet of surface area to plant roots. If 3 miles of microscopic root tips and hairs (roughly 16,000 lineal feet) draws water only from a few millimeters of surrounding soil, then that single rye plant should be able to continue ramifying into a cubic foot of silty soil and find enough water for quite a few days before wilting. These arithmetical estimates agree with my observations in the garden, and with my experiences raising transplants in pots.

LOWERED PLANT DENSITY: THE KEY TO WATER-WISE GARDENING

I always think my latest try at writing a near-perfect garden book is quite a bit better than the last. *Growing Vegetables West of the Cascades* (1989) recommended somewhat wider spacings on raised beds than I did in the first edition (1980) because I'd repeatedly noticed that once a leaf canopy forms, plant growth slows markedly. Adding a little more

Dealing with a Surprise Water Shortage

Suppose you are growing a conventional, irrigated garden and something unanticipated interrupts your ability to water. Perhaps you are homesteading and your well begins to dry up. Perhaps you're a backyard gardener and the municipality temporarily restricts usage. What to do?

First, if at all possible before the restrictions take effect, water very heavily and long to ensure there is maximum sub-soil moisture. Then eliminate all newly started interplantings and ruthlessly hoe out at least 75 percent of the remaining immature plants and about half of those about two weeks away from harvest.

For example, suppose you've got a 4-foot-wide intensive bed holding seven rows of broccoli on 12-inch centers, or about 21 plants. Remove at least every other row and every other plant in the three or four remaining rows. Try to bring plant densities down to those described in Chapter 5, "How to Grow It: A–Z."

Then shallowly hoe the soil every day or two to encourage the surface inches to dry out and form a dust mulch. You water-wise person—you're already dry gardening! Now start fertigating.

fertilizer helps after plants "bump," but still the rate of growth never equals that of younger plants. For years I assumed crowded plants stopped producing as much because competition developed for light. But now I see that unseen competition for root room also slows them down. Even if moisture is regularly recharged by irrigation, and although nutrients are replaced, once a bit of earth has been occupied by the roots of one plant it is not so readily available to the roots of another. So allocating more elbow room allows vegetables to get larger and yield longer and allows the gardener to reduce the frequency of irrigations.

Though hot, baking sun and wind can desiccate the few inches of surface soil, withdrawals of moisture from greater depths are made by growing plants transpiring moisture through their leaf surfaces. The amount of water a growing crop will transpire is determined first by the nature of the species itself, then by the amount of leaf exposed to sun, air temperature, humidity, and wind. In these respects, the crop is like an automobile radiator. With cars, the more metal surfaces, the colder the ambient air, and the higher the wind speed, the better the radiator can cool; in the garden, the more leaf surfaces, the faster, warmer, and drier the wind, and the brighter the sunlight, the more water is lost through transpiration.

How long available soil water will sustain a crop is determined by how many plants are drawing on the reserve, how extensively their root systems develop, and how many leaves are transpiring the moisture. If there are no plants, most of the water will stay unused in the barren soil through the entire growing season. If a crop canopy is established midway through the growing season, the rate of water loss will approximate that listed in the table "Estimated Irrigation Requirements," in Chapter 1. If by very close planting the crop canopy is established as early as possible and maintained by successive interplantings, as is recommended by most advocates of raised-bed gardening, water losses will greatly exceed this rate.

Many vegetable species become mildly stressed when soil moisture has dropped about half the way from capacity to the wilting point. On very closely planted beds a crop can get in serious trouble without irrigation in a matter of days. But if that same crop were planted less densely, it might grow a few weeks without irrigation. And if that crop were planted even farther apart so that no crop canopy ever developed and a considerable amount of bare, dry earth were showing, this apparent waste of growing space would result in an even slower rate of soil moisture depletion. On deep, open soil the crop might yield a respectable amount without needing any irrigation at all.

West of the Cascades we expect a rainless summer; the surprise comes that rare rainy year when the soil stays moist and we gather bucketfuls of chanterelle mushrooms in early October. Though the majority of maritime Northwest gardeners do not enjoy deep, open, moisture-retentive soils, all except those with the shallowest soil can increase their use of the free moisture nature provides and lengthen the time between irrigations. The next chapter discusses making the most of whatever soil depth you have. Most of our region's gardens can yield abundantly without any rain at all if only we reduce competition for available soil moisture, judiciously fertigate some vegetable species, and practice a few other water-wise tricks.

Would lowering plant density as much as this book suggests equally lower the yield of the plot? Surprisingly, the amount harvested does not drop proportionately. In most cases, having a plant density one-eighth of that recommended by intensive gardening advocates will result in a yield about half as great as on closely planted raised beds.

Minimizing Irrigation

CHAPTER 3

Dry though the maritime Northwest summer is, we enter the growing season with our full depth of soil at field capacity. Except on clayey soils in extraordinarily frosty, high-elevation locations, we usually can till and plant before the soil has had a chance to lose much moisture.

There are a number of things we can do to help soil moisture better sustain our summer vegetables. The most obvious step is thorough weeding. Next, we can keep the surface fluffed up with a rotary tiller or hoe during April and May, to break its capillary connection with deeper soil and accelerate the formation of a dry dust mulch. Usually, weeding forces us to do this anyway. Also, if it should rain during summer, we can hoe or rotary till a day or two later and again help a new dust mulch to develop.

BUILDING BIGGER ROOT SYSTEMS

Without irrigation, most of the plant's water supply is obtained by expansion into new earth that hasn't been desiccated by other competing roots. Eliminating any obstacles to rapid growth of root systems is the key to success. So, keep in mind a few facts about how roots grow and prosper.

The air supply in soil limits or allows root growth. Unlike the leaves, roots do not perform photosynthesis, breaking down carbon dioxide gas into atmospheric oxygen and carbon. Yet root cells must breathe oxygen. This is obtained from the air held in spaces between soil particles. Many other soil-dwelling life-forms from bacteria to moles compete for this same oxygen. Consequently, soil oxygen levels are lower than in the atmosphere. A slow exchange of gases does occur between soil air and free atmosphere, but deeper in the soil there will inevitably be less oxygen. Different plant species have varying degrees of root tolerance for lack of oxygen, but they all stop growing at some depth. Moisture reserves below the roots' maximum depth become relatively inaccessible.

Soil compaction reduces the overall supply and exchange of soil air. Compacted soil also acts as a mechanical barrier to root system expansion. When gardening with unlimited irrigation or where rain falls frequently, it is quite possible to have satisfactory growth when only the surface 6 or 7 inches of soil facilitates root development. When gardening with limited water, China's the limit, because if soil conditions permit, many vegetable species are capable of reaching 4, 5, and even 8 feet down to find moisture and nutrition.

EVALUATING POTENTIAL ROOTING ABILITY

One of the most instructive things a water-wise gardener can do is to rent or borrow a hand-operated fence post auger and bore a 3-foot-deep hole. It can be even more educational to buy a short section of ordinary water pipe to extend the auger's reach another 2 or 3 feet down. In soil free of stones, using an auger is more instructive than using a conventional posthole digger or shoveling out a small pit, because where soil is loose, the hole deepens rapidly. Where any layer is even slightly compacted, one turns and turns the bit without much effect. Augers also lift the materials more or less as they are stratified. If your soil is somewhat stony (like much upland soil north of Centralia left by the Vashon Glacier), the more usual fence-post digger or common shovel works better.

If you find more than 4 feet of soil, the site holds a dry-gardening potential that increases with the additional depth. Some soils along the floodplains of rivers or in broad valleys like the Willamette or Skagit can be over 20 feet deep, and hold far more water than the deepest roots could draw or capillary flow could raise during an entire growing season. Gently sloping land can often carry 5 to 7 feet of open, usable soil. However, soils on steep hillsides become increasingly thin and fragile with increasing slope.

Whether an urban, suburban, or rural gardener, you should make no assumptions about the depth and openness of the soil at your disposal. Dig a test hole. If you find less than 2 unfortunate feet of open earth before hitting an impermeable obstacle such as rock or gravel, not much water storage can occur and the only use this book will hold for you is to guide your move to a more likely gardening location or

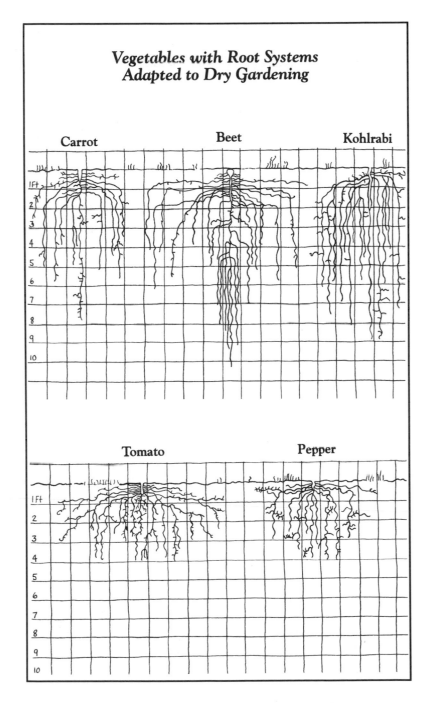

Vegetables with Root Systems Adapted to Dry Gardening

Carrot   Beet   Kohlrabi

Tomato   Pepper

encourage the house hunter to seek further. Of course, you can still garden quite successfully on thin soil in the conventional, irrigated manner. *Growing Vegetables West of the Cascades* will be an excellent guide for this type of situation.

ELIMINATING PLOWPAN

Deep though the soil may be, any restriction of root expansion greatly limits the ability of plants to aggressively find water. Soils close to rivers or on floodplains may appear loose and infinitely deep but may hide subsoil zones of droughty gravel that effectively stops root growth. Some of these conditions are correctable and some are not. A compacted subsoil or even a thin compressed layer such as plowpan may also function as a barrier. Though moisture will still rise slowly by capillarity and recharge soil above plowpan, plants obtain much more water by rooting into unoccupied, damp soil.

Plowpan is very commonly encountered by homesteaders on farm soils and may be found in suburbia too, but fortunately it is the easiest obstacle to remedy. Traditionally, American croplands have been tilled with the moldboard plow. As this implement first cuts and then flips a 6- or 7-inch-deep slice of soil over, the sole—the part supporting the plow's weight—presses heavily on the earth about 7 inches below the surface. With each subsequent plowing the plow sole rides at the same 7-inch depth and an even more compacted layer develops. Once formed, plowpan prevents the crop from rooting into the subsoil. Since winter rains leach nutrients from the topsoil and deposit them in the subsoil, plowpan prevents access to these nutrients and effectively impoverishes the field. So wise farmers periodically use a subsoil plow to fracture the pan.

Plowpan can seem as firm as a rammed-earth house; once established, it can last a long, long time. My own garden land is part of what was once an old wheat farm, one of the first homesteads of the Oregon Territory. From about 1860 through the 1930s, the field produced small grains. After wheat became unprofitable, probably because of changing market conditions and soil exhaustion, the field became an unplowed pasture. Then in the 1970s it grew daffodil bulbs, occasioning more plowing. All through the eighties my soil again rested under grass. In 1987, when I began using the land, there was still a 2-inch-thick, very hard layer starting about 7 inches down. Below 9 inches the open earth is soft as butter as far as I've ever dug.

On a garden-sized plot, plowpan or compacted subsoil is easily opened with a spading fork or a very sharp common shovel. After normal rotary tilling, either tool can fairly easily be wiggled 12 inches into the earth and small bites of plowpan loosened. Once this laborious chore is accomplished the first time, deep tillage will be far easier. In fact, it becomes so easy that I've been looking for a custom-made fork with longer tines.

CURING CLAYEY SOILS

In humid climates like ours, sandy soils may seem very open and friable on the surface but frequently hold some unpleasant subsoil surprises. Over geologic time spans, mineral grains are slowly destroyed by weak soil acids and clay is formed from the breakdown products. Then heavy winter rainfall transports these minuscule clay particles deeper into the earth, where they concentrate. It is not unusual to find a sandy topsoil underlaid with a dense, cementlike, clayey sand subsoil extending down several feet. If very impervious, a thick, dense deposition like this may be called hardpan.

The spading fork cannot cure this condition as simply as it can eliminate thin plowpan. Here is one situation where, if I had a neighbor with a large tractor and subsoil plow, I'd hire him to fracture my land 3 or 4 feet deep. Painstakingly double or even triple digging will also loosen this layer. Another possible strategy for a smaller garden would be to rent a gasoline-powered posthole auger, spread manure or compost an inch or two thick, and then bore numerous, almost adjoining holes 4 feet deep all over the garden.

Clayey subsoil can supply surprisingly larger amounts of moisture than the granular sandy surface might imply, but only if the earth is opened deeply and becomes more accessible to root growth. Fortunately, once root development increases at greater depths, the organic matter content and accessibility of this clayey layer can be maintained through intelligent green manuring, postponing for years the need to subsoil again. Green manuring is discussed in detail shortly.

Other sites may have gooey, very fine clay topsoils, almost inevitably with gooey, very fine clay subsoils as well. Though incorporation of extraordinarily large quantities of organic matter can turn the top few inches into something that behaves a little like loam, it is quite impractical to work in humus to a depth of 4 or 5 feet. Root development will still be limited to the surface layer. Very fine clays don't make likely dry gardens.

Not all clay soils are "fine clay soils," totally compacted and airless. For example, on the gentler slopes of the geologic old Cascades, those 50-million-year-old black basalts that form the Cascades foothills and appear in other places throughout the maritime Northwest, a deep, friable, red clay soil called (in Oregon) Jori often forms. Jori clays can be 6 to 8 feet deep and are sufficiently porous and well drained to have been used for highly productive orchard crops. Water-wise gardeners can do wonders with Joris and other similar soils, though clays never grow the most perfectly shaped carrots and parsnips.

SPOTTING A LIKELY SITE

Observing the condition of wild plants can reveal a good site to garden without much irrigation. Where Himalaya or Evergreen blackberries grow 2 feet tall and produce small, dull-tasting fruit, there is not much available soil moisture. Where they grow 6 feet tall and the berries are sweet and good sized, there is deep, open soil. When the berry vines are 8 or more feet tall and the fruits are especially huge, usually there is both deep, loose soil and a higher than usual amount of fertility.

Other native vegetation can also reveal a lot about soil moisture reserves. For years I wondered at the short leaders and sad appearance of Douglas fir in the vicinity of Yelm, Washington. Were they due to extreme soil infertility? Then I learned that conifer trees respond more to summertime soil moisture than to fertility. I obtained a soil survey of Thurston County and discovered that much of that area was very sandy with gravelly subsoil. Eureka!

The Soil Conservation Service (SCS), a U.S. Government agency, has probably put a soil auger into your very land or a plot close by. Its tests have been correlated and mapped; the soils underlying the maritime Northwest have been named and categorized by texture, depth, and ability to provide available moisture. The maps are precise and detailed enough to approximately locate a city or suburban lot. In 1987, when I was in the market for a new homestead, I first went to my county SCS office, mapped out locations where the soil was suitable, and then went hunting. Most counties have their own office.

USING HUMUS TO INCREASE SOIL MOISTURE

Maintaining topsoil humus content in the 4 to 5 percent range is vital to plant health, vital to growing more nutritious food, and essential to bringing the soil into that state of easy workability and cooperation known as good tilth. Humus is a spongy substance capable of holding several times more available moisture than clay. There are also new synthetic, long-lasting soil amendments that hold and release even more moisture than humus. Garden books frequently recommend tilling in extraordinarily large amounts of organic matter to increase a soil's water-holding capacity in the top few inches.

Humus can improve many aspects of soil but will not reduce a garden's overall need for irrigation, because it is simply not practical to maintain sufficient humus deeply enough. Rotary tilling only blends amendments into the top 6 or 7 inches of soil. Rigorous double digging by actually trenching out 12 inches and then spading up the next foot theoretically allows one to mix in significant amounts of organic matter to nearly 24 inches. But plants can use water from far deeper than that. Let's realistically consider how much soil moisture reserves might be increased by double digging and incorporating large quantities of organic matter.

A healthy topsoil organic-matter level in our climate is about 4 percent. This rapidly declines to less than 0.5 percent in the subsoil. Suppose inches-thick layers of compost were spread and, by double digging, the organic matter content of a very sandy soil were amended to 10 percent down to 2 feet. If that soil contained little clay, its water-holding ability in the top 2 feet could be doubled. Referring to the chart "Available Moisture" in Chapter 2, we see that sandy soil can release up to 1 inch of water per foot. By dint of massive amendment we might add 1 inch of available moisture per foot of soil to the reserve. That's 2 extra inches of water, enough to increase the time an ordinary garden can last between heavy irrigations by a week or 10 days.

If the soil in question were a silty clay, it would naturally make 2½ inches available per foot. A massive humus amendment would increase that to 3½ inches in the top foot or two, relatively not as much benefit as in sandy soil. And I seriously doubt that many gardeners would be willing to thoroughly double dig to an honest 24 inches.

Trying to maintain organic matter levels above 10 percent is an almost self-defeating process. The higher the humus level gets, the more rapidly organic matter tends to decay. Finding or making enough well-finished compost to cover the garden several inches deep (what it takes to lift humus levels to 10 percent) is enough of a job. Double digging just as much more into the second foot is even more effort. But having to repeat that chore every year or two becomes downright discouraging. No, either your soil naturally holds enough moisture to permit dry gardening, or it doesn't.

KEEPING THE SUBSOIL OPEN WITH GREEN MANURING

When roots decay, fresh organic matter and large, long-lasting passageways can be left deep in the soil, allowing easier air movement and facilitating entry of other roots. But no cover crop that I am aware of will effectively penetrate firm plowpan or other resistant physical obstacles. Such a barrier forces all plants to root almost exclusively in the topsoil. However, once the subsoil has been mechanically fractured the first time, and if recompaction is avoided by shunning heavy tractors and other machinery, green manure crops can maintain the openness of the subsoil.

To accomplish this, correct green manure species selection is essential. Lawn grasses tend to be shallow rooting, while most regionally adapted pasture grasses can reach down about 3 feet at best. However, orchard grass (called coltsfoot in English farming books) will grow down 4 or more feet while leaving a massive amount of decaying organic matter in the subsoil after the sod is tilled in. Sweet clover, a biennial legume that sprouts one spring then winters over to bloom the next summer, may go down 8 feet. Red clover, a perennial species, may thickly invade the top 5 feet. Other useful subsoil busters include densely sown Umbelliferae such as carrots, parsley, and parsnip. The chicory family also makes very large and penetrating taproots.

Though seed for wild chicory is hard to obtain, cheap varieties of endive (a semicivilized relative) are easily available. And several pounds of your own excellent parsley or parsnip seed can be easily produced by letting about 10 row feet of overwintering roots form seed. Orchard grass and red clover can be had quite inexpensively at many farm supply stores. Sweet clover is not currently grown by our region's farmers and so can only be found by mail from Johnny's Selected Seeds (see Chapter 5, "How to Grow It: A–Z," for their address). Poppy seed

All photographs in this insert were taken in late July. **Top**: Dry gardened Gold Nugget tomatoes for lunch. **Bottom left**: Romaine lettuce grows great during a hot summer—if it gets lots of water. **Bottom right**: Westland Winter Kale, tomatoes, and sunflowers. The row- and between-row spacing is about 4 feet. (GREG LAWLER/ SMALL PLANET PHOTOGRAPHY)

Top: Eggplants already! Notice the cloche support. The plastic tunnel was removed over a month earlier. **Bottom left**: Golden zucchini raised with abundant fertigation. **Bottom right**: Carrots thinned to a foot apart. By October the carrots were 3 to 5 inches in diameter and a foot long. (GREG LAWLER/SMALL PLANET PHOTOGRAPHY)

Top: Unirrigated Red Russian Kale thrives, but weaker-rooted Brussels sprouts are stunted. The endive plants in the foreground grew crowded and lush by September, without rain or fertigation. **Bottom:** The Naan sprinkers spray only as far as the bush beans on my left. The summer squash beyond their reach are fertigated. (GREG LAWLER/ SMALL PLANET PHOTOGRAPHY)

Steve's 1992 Garden Plan *(planting times are indicated by color)*

Row #	
6	Overwintered Cauliflower Transplants ··· Tomatoes ··· Peppers ··· Eggplant
5	Early Peas ··· Sorrel ··· Parsley ··· Endive ··· Giant Kohlrabi
4	Beets ··· Carrots
3	Olrasa Kale ··· Napa Kale
2	Savoy Cabbage ··· Brussels Sprouts
1	Rutabagas ··· Early Zucchini ··· Leek Transplants
	Lettuce & Spinach

Raised Bed:

Spinach & Lettuce / Spinach & Lettuce	Spinach & Lettuce / Lettuce & Arugula	Lettuce	Celery	Kohlrabi	Leek Nursery	Overwintering Onion & Winter Scallion Nursery	Overwintering Cauliflower & Cabbage Nursery	Chinese Cabbage

Row #	
7	Broccoli ··· Arugula ··· Broccoli ··· Broccoli ··· Late Cauliflower
8	Pole Peas ··· Purple Sprouting Broccoli ··· Pole Beans
9	Winter & Summer Squash ··· Cucumber ··· Melons / Spring Cabbage ··· Scallions
10	Early Potatoes ··· Main Season Potatoes

60'

125'

Legend: ■ Early Spring ■ Midspring ■ Late Spring ■ Midsummer ■ Late Summer ⊗ Sprinklers ▨ Sprinkler Application used for cooking will often sprout. Sown densely in October, it forms a thick carpet of frilly spring greens underlaid with countless massive taproots that decompose very rapidly if the plants are tilled in in April before flower stalks begin to appear. If you're using poppies as a green manure crop, beware of trouble with the DEA or other authorities. I'd be sure to till them in before their beautiful blossoms attract unwarranted attention.

For country gardeners, the best rotations include several years of perennial grass-legume-herb mixtures to maintain the openness of the subsoil followed by a few years of vegetables and then back (see Frank Newman Turner's book in More Reading). I plan my own garden this way. In October, after a few inches of rain has softened the earth, I spread 50 pounds of agricultural lime per 1,000 square feet and break the thick pasture sod covering next year's garden plot by shallow rotary tilling. Early the next spring I broadcast a concoction I call "complete organic fertilizer" (see *Growing Vegetables West of the Cascades* or the Territorial Seed Company catalog), till again after the soil dries down a bit, and then use a spading fork to open the subsoil before making a seedbed. The first time around, I had to break the century-old plowpan —forking compacted earth a foot deep is a lot of work. In subsequent rotations it is much, much easier.

For a couple of years, vegetables will grow vigorously on this new ground supported only with a complete organic fertilizer. But vegetable gardening makes humus levels decline rapidly. So every few years I start a new garden on another plot and replant the old garden to green manures. I never remove vegetation during the long rebuilding under green manures, but merely mow it once or twice a year and allow the organic matter content of the soil to redevelop. If there ever were a place where chemical fertilizers might be appropriate around a garden, it would be to affordably enhance the growth of biomass during green manuring.

Were I a serious city vegetable gardener, I'd consider growing vegetables in the front yard for a few years and then switching to the back yard. Having lots of space, as I do now, I keep three or four garden plots available, one in vegetables and the others restoring their organic matter content under grass.

MULCHING

Gardening under a permanent thick mulch of crude organic matter is recommended by Ruth Stout (see the listing for her book in More Reading) and her disciples as a surefire way to drought-proof gardens while eliminating virtually any need for tillage, weeding, and fertilizing. I have attempted the method in both Southern California and western Oregon—with disastrous results in both locations. What follows in this section is addressed to gardeners who have already read glowing reports about mulching.

Permanent mulching with vegetation actually does not reduce summertime moisture loss any better than mulching with dry soil, sometimes called "dust mulching." In fact, while the surface layer stays moist, water will steadily be wicked up by capillarity and be evaporated from the soil's surface. If frequent light sprinkling keeps the surface perpetually moist, subsoil moisture loss can occur all summer, so un-mulched soil could eventually become desiccated many feet deep. However, capillary movement only happens when soil is damp. Once even a thin layer of soil has become quite dry it almost completely prevents any further movement. West of the Cascades, this happens all by itself in late spring. One hot, sunny day follows another, and soon the earth's surface seems parched.

Unfortunately, by the time a dusty layer forms, quite a bit of soil water may have risen from the depths and been lost. The gardener can significantly reduce spring moisture loss by frequently hoeing weeds until the top inch or two of earth is dry and powdery. This effort will probably be necessary in any case, because weeds will germinate prolifically until the surface layer is sufficiently desiccated. On the off chance it should rain hard during summer, it is very wise to again hoe a few times to rapidly restore the dust mulch. If hand cultivation seems very hard work, I suggest you learn to sharpen your hoe.

A mulch of dry hay, grass clippings, leaves, and the like will also retard rapid surface evaporation. Gardeners think mulching prevents moisture loss better than bare earth because under mulch the soil stays damp right to the surface. However, dig down 4 to 6 inches under a dust mulch and the earth is just as damp as under hay. And soil moisture studies have proved that overall moisture loss using vegetation mulch slightly exceeds loss under a dust mulch.

West of the Cascades, the question of which method is superior is a bit complex, with pros and cons on both sides. Without a long winter freeze to set populations back, permanent thick mulch quickly breeds so many slugs, earwigs, and sowbugs that it cannot be maintained for more than one year before vegetable gardening becomes very difficult. Laying down a fairly thin mulch in June after the soil has warmed up well, raking up what remains of the mulch early the next spring, and composting it prevents destructive insect population levels from developing while simultaneously reducing surface compaction by winter rains and beneficially enhancing the survival and multiplication of earthworms. But a thin mulch also enhances the summer germination of weed seeds without being thick enough to suppress their emergence. And any mulch, even a thin one, makes hoeing virtually impossible, while hand weeding through mulch is tedious.

Mulch has some unqualified pluses in hotter climates. Most of the organic matter in soil and consequently most of the available nitrogen is found in the surface few inches. Levels of other available mineral nutrients are usually two or three times as high in the topsoil as well. However, if the surface few inches of soil becomes completely desiccated, no root activity will occur there and the plants are forced to feed deeper, in soil far less fertile. Keeping the topsoil damp does greatly improve the growth of some shallow-feeding species such as lettuce and radishes. But with our climate's cool nights, most vegetables need the soil as warm as possible, and the cooling effect of mulch can be as much a hindrance as a help. I've tried mulching quite a few species while dry gardening and found little or no improvement in plant growth with most of them. Probably, the enhancement of nutrition compensates for the harm from lowering soil temperature. Fertigation is better all around.

WINDBREAKS

Plants transpire more moisture when the sun shines, when temperatures are high, and when the wind blows; it is just like drying laundry. Windbreaks also help the garden grow in winter by increasing temperature. Many other garden books discuss windbreaks, and I conclude that I have a better use for the small amount of words my publisher allows me than to repeat this data; Binda Colebrook's *Winter Gardening in the Maritime Northwest* (Sasquatch Books, 1989) is especially good on this topic.

Increasing Soil Fertility Saves Water

Does crop growth equal water use? Most people would say this statement seems likely to be true.

Actually, faster-growing crops use much less soil moisture than slower-growing ones. As early as 1882 it was determined that less water is required to produce a pound of plant matter when the soil is fertilized than when it is not fertilized. One experiment required 1,100 pounds of water to grow 1 pound of dry matter on infertile soil, but only 575 pounds of water to produce a pound of dry matter on rich land. Perhaps the single most important thing a water-wise gardener can do is increase the fertility of the soil, especially the subsoil.

Poor plant nutrition increases the water cost of every pound of dry matter produced.

FERTILIZING, FOLIAR FEEDING, AND FERTIGATING

In our heavily leached region almost no soil is naturally rich, while fertilizers, manures, and potent composts mainly improve the topsoil. But the water-wise gardener must get nutrition down deep, where the soil stays damp through the summer.

If plants with enough remaining elbow room stop growing in summer and begin to appear gnarly, it is just as likely due to lack of nutrition as lack of water. Several things can be done to limit or prevent midsummer stunting. First, before sowing or transplanting large species like tomato, squash, or big brassicas, dig out a small pit about 12 inches deep and below that blend in a handful or two of organic fertilizer. Then fill the hole back in. This double-digging process blends concentrated fertility into the soil 18 to 24 inches below the seeds or seedlings.

Foliar feeding is another water-wise technique that keeps plants growing through the summer. Soluble nutrients sprayed on plant leaves are rapidly absorbed into the vascular system. Unfortunately, dilute nutrient solutions that won't burn leaves only provoke a strong growth response for 3 to 5 days. Optimally, foliar nutrition must be applied weekly or even more frequently. To efficiently spray a garden larger than a few hundred square feet, I suggest buying an industrial-grade, 3-gallon backpack sprayer with a side-handle pump. Approximate cost as of this writing was $80. The store that sells it (probably a farm supply store) will also support you with a complete assortment of inexpensive nozzles that can vary the rate of emission and the spray pattern. High-quality equipment like this outlasts many, many cheaper and smaller sprayers designed for the consumer market, and replacement parts are also available. Keep in mind that consumer merchandise is designed to be consumed; stuff made for farming is built to last.

Using foliar fertilizers requires a little caution and forethought. Spinach, beet, and chard leaves seem particularly sensitive to foliars (and even to organic insecticides) and may be damaged by even half-strength applications. And the cabbage family coats its leaf surfaces with a waxy, moisture-retentive sealant that makes sprays bead up and run off rather than stick and be absorbed. Mixing foliar feed solutions with a little spreader/sticker, Safer's Soap, or, if bugs are also a problem, with a liquid organic insecticide like Red Arrow (a pyrethrum-rotenone mix), eliminates surface tension and allows the fertilizer to have an effect on brassicas.

Sadly, in terms of nutrient balance, the poorest foliar sprays are organic. That's because it is nearly impossible to get significant quantities of phosphorus or calcium into solution using any combination of fish emulsion and seaweed or liquid kelp. The most useful possible organic foliar is made by combining ½ to 1 tablespoon each of fish emulsion and liquid seaweed concentrate per gallon of water.

Foliar spraying and fertigation (watering with extra-fertilized water) are two occasions when I am comfortable supplementing my organic fertilizers with water-soluble chemical fertilizers. The best and most expensive brand is Rapid-Gro. Less costly concoctions, such as Peters 20-20-20 or the other "Grows," don't provide as complete trace mineral support or use as many sources of nutrition. One thing fertilizer makers find expensive to accomplish is concocting a mixture of soluble nutrients that also contains calcium, a vital plant food. If you dissolve calcium nitrate into a solution containing other soluble plant nutrients, many of them will precipitate out because few calcium compounds are soluble. Even Rapid-Gro doesn't attempt to supply calcium. Recently I've discovered better-quality hydroponic nutrient solutions that do use chemicals that provide soluble calcium. These also make excellent foliar sprays. Brands of hydroponic nutrient solutions seem to appear and vanish rapidly. I've had great luck with Dyna-Gro 7-9-5. All these chemicals are mixed at about 1 tablespoon per gallon.

Vegetables That:

Like foliars

Asparagus	Carrots	Melons	Squash
Beans	Cauliflower	Peas	Tomatoes
Broccoli	Cucumbers	Potatoes	
Brussels sprouts	Eggplant	Radishes	
Cabbage	Kale	Rutabagas	

Don't like foliars

Beets	Leeks	Onions	Spinach
Chard	Lettuce	Peppers	

Like fertigation

Brussels sprouts	Kale	Savoy cabbage
Cucumbers	Melons	Squash
Eggplant	Peppers	Tomatoes

Fertigation every two to four weeks is the best technique for maximizing yield while minimizing water use. I usually make my first fertigation late in June and continue periodically through early September. I use six or seven plastic 5-gallon "drip system" buckets (see below), setting one by each plant, and filling them all with a hose each time I work in the garden. Doing 12 or 14 plants each time I'm in the garden, it takes no special effort to rotate through the entire garden more or less every three weeks.

To make a drip bucket, drill a 3/16-inch hole through the side of a 4- to 6-gallon plastic bucket about 1/4-inch up from the bottom, or in the bottom at the edge. The empty bucket is placed so that the fertilized water drains out close to the stem of a plant. It is then filled with liquid fertilizer solution. It takes 5 to 10 minutes for 5 gallons to pass through a small opening, and because of the slow flow rate, water penetrates deeply into the subsoil without wetting much of the surface. Each fertigation makes the plant grow very rapidly for two to three weeks, more I suspect as a result of improved nutrition than from added moisture. Exactly how and when to fertigate each species is explained in Chapter 5.

Organic gardeners may fertigate with combinations of fish emulsion and seaweed at the same dilution used for foliar spraying, or with compost/manure tea. Determining the correct strength to make compost tea is a matter of trial and error. I usually rely on weak Rapid-Gro mixed at half the recommended dilution. The strength of the fertilizer you need depends on how much and deeply you placed nutrition in the subsoil.

Water-Wise Year-Round

CHAPTER 4

EARLY SPRING:
THE EASIEST UNWATERED GARDEN

West of the Cascades, most crops started in February and March require
no special handling when irrigation is scarce. These include peas, early
lettuce, radishes, kohlrabi, early broccoli, and so forth. However, some
of these vegetables are harvested as late as June, so to reduce their need
for irrigation, space them wider than usual. Spring vegetables also will
exhaust most of the moisture from the soil before maturing, making
succession planting impossible without first irrigating heavily. Early
spring plantings are best allocated one of two places in the garden plan:
either in that part of the garden that will be fully irrigated all summer
or in a part of a big garden that can affordably remain bare during
the summer and be used in October for receiving transplants of overwintering crops. The garden plan and discussion in Chapter 6 illustrate
these ideas in detail.

LATER IN SPRING:
SPROUTING SEEDS WITHOUT WATERING

For the first years that I experimented with dry gardening I went over-
board and attempted to grow food as though I had no running water at
all. The greatest difficulty caused by this self-imposed handicap was
sowing small-seeded species after the season warmed up.

Sprouting what we in the seed business call "big seed"—corn,
beans, peas, squash, cucumbers, and melons—is relatively easy without
irrigation because these crops are planted deeply, where soil moisture
still resides long after the surface has dried out. And even if it is so late
in the season that the surface has become very dry, a wide, shallow
ditch made with a shovel will expose moist soil several inches down. A

41

Handmade Footprints

Sometimes I sow large brassicas and cucurbits in clumps above a fertilized, double-dug spot. First, in a space about 18 inches square, I deeply dig in complete organic fertilizer. Then with my fist I punch down a depression in the center of the fluffed-up mound. Sometimes my fist goes in so easily that I have to replace a little more soil and punch it down some more. The purpose is not to make rammed earth or cement, but only to reestablish capillarity by having firm soil under a shallow, fist-sized depression. Then a pinch of seed is sprinkled atop this depression and covered with fine earth. Even if several hot, sunny days follow I get good germination without watering. This same technique works excellently on hills of squash, melon, and cucumber as well, though these large-seeded species must be planted quite a bit deeper.

furrow can be cut in the bottom of that damp "valley" and big seeds germinated with little or no watering.

Tillage breaks capillary connections until the fluffy soil resettles. This interruption is useful for preventing moisture loss in summer, but the same phenomenon makes the surface dry out in a flash. In recently tilled earth, successfully sprouting small seeds in warm weather is dicey without frequent watering.

With a bit of forethought, the water-wise gardener can easily reestablish capillarity below sprouting seeds so that moisture held deeper in the soil rises to replace that lost from surface layers, reducing or eliminating the need for watering. The principle here can be easily demonstrated. In fact, there probably isn't any gardener who has not seen the phenomenon at work without realizing it. Every gardener has tilled the soil, gone out the next morning, and noticed that his or her compacted footprints were moist while the rest of the earth was dry and fluffy. Foot pressure restored capillarity, and during the night, fresh moisture replaced what had evaporated.

This simple technique helps start everything except carrots and parsnips (which must have completely loose soil to develop correctly). All the gardener must do is intentionally compress the soil below the seeds and then cover the seeds with a mulch of loose, dry soil. Sprouting seeds then rest atop damp soil exactly as they lie on a damp blotter in a germination laboratory's covered petri dish. This dampness will not disappear before the sprouting seedling has propelled a root several inches farther down and is putting a leaf into the sunlight.

I've used several techniques to reestablish capillarity after tilling. There's a wise old plastic push planter in my garage that first compacts the tilled earth with its front wheel, cuts a furrow, drops the seed, and then with its drag chain pulls loose soil over the furrow. I've also pulled one wheel of a garden cart or pushed a lightly loaded wheelbarrow down the row to press down a wheel track, sprinkled seed on that compacted furrow, and then pulled loose soil over it.

SUMMER: HOW TO FLUID DRILL SEEDS

Soaking seeds before sowing is another water-wise technique, especially useful later in the season. At bedtime, place the seeds in a half-pint mason jar, cover with a square of plastic window screen held on with a strong rubber band, soak the seeds overnight, and then drain them first thing in the morning. Gently rinse the seeds with cool water two or three times daily until the root tips begin to emerge. As soon as this sign appears, the seed must be sown, because the newly emerging roots become increasingly subject to breaking off as they develop and soon form tangled masses. Presprouted seeds may be gently blended into some crumbly, moist soil and this mixture gently sprinkled into a furrow and covered. If the sprouts are particularly delicate or, as with carrots, you want a very uniform stand, disperse the seeds in a starch gelatin and imitate what commercial vegetable growers call fluid drilling.

Heat one pint of water to the boiling point. Dissolve in 2 to 3 tablespoons of ordinary cornstarch. Place the mixture in the refrigerator to cool. Soon the liquid will become a soupy gel. Gently mix this cool starch gel with the sprouting seeds, making sure the seeds are uniformly blended. Pour the mixture into a 1-quart plastic zipper bag and, scissors in hand, go out to the garden. After a furrow—with capillarity restored—has been prepared, cut a small hole in one lower corner of the plastic bag. The hole size should be under ¼ inch in diameter. Walk quickly down the row, dribbling a mixture of gel and seeds into the furrow. Then cover. You may have to experiment a few times with cooled gel minus seeds until you divine the proper hole size, walking speed, and amount of gel needed per length of furrow. Not only will presprouted seeds come up days sooner, and not only will the root be penetrating moist soil long before the shoot emerges, but the stand of seedlings will be very uniformly spaced and easier to thin. After fluid drilling a few times you'll realize that one needs quite a bit less seed per length of row than you previously thought.

ESTABLISHING THE FALL AND WINTER GARDEN

West of the Cascades, germinating fall and winter crops in the heat of summer is always difficult. Even when the entire garden is well watered, midsummer sowings require daily attention and frequent sprinkling; however, once they have germinated, keeping little seedlings growing in an irrigated garden usually requires no more water than the rest of the garden gets. But once hot weather comes, establishing small seeds in the dry garden seems next to impossible without regular watering. Should a lucky, perfectly timed, and unusually heavy summer rainfall sprout your seeds, they still would not grow well because the next few inches of soil would at best be only slightly moist.

A related problem many backyard gardeners have with establishing the winter and overwintered garden is finding enough space for both the summer and winter crops. The nursery bed solves both these problems. Instead of trying to irrigate the entire area that will eventually be occupied by a winter or overwintered crop at maturity, the seedlings are first grown in irrigated nurseries for transplanting in autumn after the rains come back. Were I desperately short of water I'd locate my nursery where it got only morning sun and sow a week or 10 days earlier to compensate for the slower growth.

Vegetables to Start in a Nursery Bed

Variety	Sowing date	Transplanting date
Fall/winter lettuce	mid-August	early October
Leeks	early April	July
Overwintered onions	early–mid-August	December/January
Spring cabbage	mid–late August	November/December
Spring cauliflower	mid-August	October/November
Winter scallions	mid-July	mid-October

Seedlings in pots and trays are hard to keep moist and require daily tending. Fortunately, growing transplants in little pots is not necessary because in autumn, when they'll be set out, humidity is high, temperatures are cool, the sun is weak, and transpiration losses are minimal, so seedling transplants will tolerate considerable root loss. My nursery is sown in rows about 8 inches apart across a raised bed and thinned gradually to prevent crowding, because crowded seedlings are hard to dig out without damage. When the prediction of a few days of cloudy weather encourages transplanting, the seedlings are lifted with a large, sharp knife. If the fall rains are late and/or the crowded seedlings are getting leggy, a relatively small amount of irrigation will moisten the planting areas. Another light watering at transplanting time will almost certainly establish the seedlings quite successfully. And, finding room for these crops ceases to be a problem because fall transplants can be set out as a succession crop following hot weather vegetables such as squash, melons, cucumbers, tomatoes, potatoes, and beans.

Vegetables That Must Be Heavily Irrigated
(*These crops are not suitable for dry gardens.*)

Bulb onions (for fall harvest)
Celeriac
Celery
Chinese cabbage
Lettuce (summer and fall)
Radishes (summer and fall)
Scallions (for summer harvest)
Spinach (summer)

How to Grow It: A–Z

CHAPTER 5

FIRST, A WORD ABOUT VARIETIES

As recently as the 1930s, most American country folk still did not have running water. With water being hand-pumped and carried in buckets, and precious, their vegetable gardens had to be grown with a minimum of irrigation. In the otherwise well-watered East, one could routinely expect several consecutive weeks every summer without rain. In some drought years a hot, rainless month or longer could go by. So vegetable varieties were bred to grow through dry spells without loss, and traditional American vegetable gardens were designed to help them do so.

I began gardening in the early 1970s, just as the raised-bed method was being popularized. The latest books and magazine articles all agreed that raising vegetables in widely separated single rows was a foolish imitation of commercial farming, that commercial vegetables were arranged that way for ease of mechanical cultivation. Closely planted raised beds requiring hand cultivation were alleged to be far more productive and far more efficient users of irrigation because water wasn't evaporating from bare soil.

I think this is more likely to be the truth: Old-fashioned gardens used low plant densities to survive inevitable spells of rainlessness. Looked at this way, widely separated vegetables in widely separated rows may be considered the more efficient users of water because they consume soil moisture that nature freely puts there. Only after, and if, these reserves are significantly depleted does the gardener have to irrigate. The end result is surprisingly more abundant than a modern gardener educated on intensive, raised-bed propaganda would think.

Finding varieties still adapted to water-wise gardening is becoming difficult. Most American vegetables are now bred for irrigation-dependent California. Like raised-bed gardeners, vegetable farmers

47

Seed Company Directory*

ABUNDANT LIFE SEED FOUNDATION: P.O. Box 772, Port Townsend, WA 98368 (ABL)

JOHNNY'S SELECTED SEEDS: Foss Hill Road, Albion, Maine 04910 (JSS)

PEACE SEEDS: 2345 SE Thompson Street, Corvallis, OR 97333 (PEA)

RONNINGER'S SEED POTATOES: Star Route, Moyie Springs, Idaho 83845 (RSP)

STOKES SEEDS INC. Box 548, Buffalo, NY 14240 (STK)

TERRITORIAL SEED COMPANY, P.O. Box 20, Cottage Grove, OR 97424 (TSC)

*Throughout the growing directions provided in this chapter, the reader will be referred to a specific company only for varieties that are not widely available.

have discovered that they can make a bigger profit by growing smaller, quick-maturing plants in high-density spacings. Most modern vegetables have been bred to suit this method. Many new varieties can't forage and have become smaller, more determinate, and faster to mature. Actually, the larger, more sprawling heirloom varieties of the past were not a great deal less productive overall, but only a little later to begin yielding.

Fortunately, enough of the old sorts still exist that a selective and varietally aware home gardener can make do. Since I've become water-wiser, I'm interested in finding and conserving heirlooms that once supported large numbers of healthy Americans in relative self-sufficiency. My earlier book, being a guide to what passes for ordinary vegetable gardening these days, assumed the availability of plenty of water. The varieties I recommended in *Growing Vegetables West of the Cascades* were largely modern ones, and the seed companies I praised most highly focused on top-quality commercial varieties. But, looking at gardening through the filter of limited irrigation, other, less modern varieties are often far better adapted and other seed companies sometimes more likely sources.

I have again come to appreciate the older style of vegetable—sprawling, large framed, later maturing, longer yielding, vigorously rooting. However, many of these old-timers have not seen the attentions of a professional plant breeder for many years and throw a fair percentage of bizarre, misshapen, nonproductive plants. These "off types" can be compensated for by growing a somewhat larger garden and allowing for some waste. Dr. Alan Kapuler, who runs Peace Seeds, has brilliantly pointed out to me why heirloom varieties are likely to be more nutritious. Propagated by centuries of isolated homesteaders, heirlooms that survived did so because these superior varieties helped the gardeners' better-nourished babies pass through the gauntlet of childhood illnesses.

PLANT SPACING

Reduced plant density is the essence of dry gardening. The recommended spacings in this section are those I have found workable at Elkton, Oregon. My dry garden is generally laid out in single rows, the row centers 4 feet apart. Some larger crops, like potatoes, tomatoes, beans, and cucurbits (squash, cucumbers, and melons), are allocated more elbow room. Those few species requiring intensive irrigation are grown on a heavily watered raised bed, tightly spaced. I cannot prescribe what would be the perfect, most efficient spacing for your garden. Are your temperatures lower than mine and evaporation less? Or is your weather hotter? Does your soil hold more than, less than, or just as much available moisture as mine? Is it as deep and open and moisture retentive?

To help you compare your site with mine, I give you the following data. My homestead is only 25 miles inland and is always several degrees cooler in summer than the Willamette Valley. Washingtonians and British Columbians have even cooler days and a greater likelihood of significant summertime rain and so may plant a little closer together. Inland gardeners farther south or in the Willamette Valley may want to spread their plants out a little farther.

Living on 16 acres, I have virtually unlimited space to garden in. The focus of my recent research has been to eliminate irrigation as much as possible while maintaining food quality. Those with thinner soil who are going to depend more on fertigation may plant closer, how close depending on the amount of water available. More irrigation will also give higher per-square-foot yields.

Whatever your combination of conditions, your results can only be determined by trial. I'd suggest you become water-wise by testing a range of spacings.

WHEN TO PLANT

If you've already been growing an irrigated year-round garden, this book's suggested planting dates may surprise you. And as with spacing, sowing dates must also be wisely adjusted to your location. The planting dates in this chapter are what I follow in my own garden. It is impractical to include specific dates for all the microclimatic areas of the maritime Northwest and for every vegetable species. Readers are asked to make adjustments by understanding their weather relative to mine.

Gardeners to the north of me and at higher elevations should make their spring sowings a week or two later than the dates I use. In

Adjusting Planting Dates

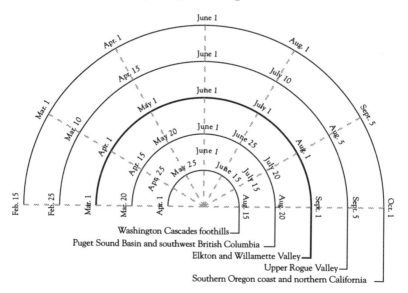

Washington Cascades foothills ⌐
Puget Sound Basin and southwest British Columbia ⌐
Elkton and Willamette Valley ⌐
Upper Rogue Valley ⌐
Southern Oregon coast and northern California ⌐

the Garden Valley of Roseburg and south along I-5, start spring plantings a week or two earlier. Along the southern Oregon coast and in northern California, start three or four weeks sooner than I do.

Fall comes earlier to the north of me and to higher-elevation gardens; end-of-season growth rates there also slow more profoundly than they do at Elkton. Summers are cooler along the coast; that has the same effect of slowing late-summer growth. Items started after midsummer should be given one or two extra growing weeks by coastal, high-elevation, and northern gardeners. Gardeners to the south should sow their late crops a week or two later than I do; along the south Oregon coast and in northern California, two to four weeks later than I do.

Arugula (Rocket)

The tender, peppery little leaves make winter salads much more interesting and tasty.

SOWING DATE: I delay sowing until late August or early September so my crowded patch of arugula lasts all winter and doesn't make seed until March. Pregerminated seeds emerge fast and strong. Sprouted in early October, arugula still may reach eating size in midwinter.

SPACING: Thinly seed a row into any vacant niche. The seedlings will be insignificantly small until late summer.

IRRIGATION: If the seedlings suffer a bit from moisture stress they'll catch up rapidly when the fall rains begin.

VARIETIES: None.

Beans of All Sorts

Heirloom pole beans once climbed over considerable competition while vigorously struggling for water, nutrition, and light. Modern bush varieties tend to have puny root systems.

SOWING DATE: Mid-April is the usual time on the Umpqua; elsewhere, sow after the danger of frost is over and soil stays over 60°F. If the earth is getting dry by this date, soak the seed overnight before sowing and furrow down to moist soil. However, do not cover the seeds more than 2 inches.

SPACING: Twelve to 16 inches apart at final thinning. Allow about 2½ to 3 feet on either side of the trellis to avoid root competition from other plants.

IRRIGATION: If part of the garden is sprinkler irrigated, space beans a little tighter and locate the bean trellis toward the outer reach of the sprinkler's throw. Due to its height, the trellis tends to intercept quite a bit of water and dumps it at the base. You can also use the bucket-drip method and fertigate the beans, giving about 25 gallons per 10 row-feet once or twice during the summer. Pole beans can make a meaningful yield without any irrigation; under severe moisture stress they will survive, but bear little.

VARIETIES: Any of the pole types seem to do fine. Runner beans seem to prefer cooler locations but are every bit as drought tolerant as ordinary snap beans. My current favorites are Kentucky Wonder White Seeded, Fortrex (TSC, JSS), and Musica (TSC).

The older heirloom dry beans were mostly pole types. They are reasonably productive if allowed to sprawl on the ground without support. Their unirrigated seed yield is lower, but the seed is still plump, tastes great, and sprouts well. Compared with unirrigated Black Coco (TSC), which is my most productive and best-tasting bush cultivar, Kentucky Wonder Brown Seeded (sometimes called Old Homestead) (STK, PEA, ABL) yields about 50 percent more seed and keeps on growing for weeks after Coco has quit. Do not bother to fertigate untrellised pole beans grown for dry seed. With the threat of September moisture always looming over dry bean plots, we need to encourage vines to quit setting and dry down. Peace Seeds and Abundant Life offer long lists of heirloom vining dry bean varieties.

Serious self-sufficiency buffs seeking to produce their own legume supply should also consider the fava, garbanzo bean, and Alaska pea. Many favas can be overwintered: sow in October, sprout on fall rains, grow over the winter, and dry down in June with the soil. Garbanzos are grown like mildly frost-tolerant peas. Alaska peas are the type used for pea soup. They're spring sown and grown like ordinary shelling peas. Avoid overhead irrigation while seeds are drying down.

Beets

Beets will root far deeper and wider than most people realize—in uncompacted, nonacid soils. Double or triple dig the subsoil directly below the seed row.

SOWING DATE: Early April at Elkton, late March farther south, and as late as April 30 in British Columbia. Beet seed germinates easily in moist, cool soil. A single sowing may be harvested from June through early March the next year. If properly thinned, good varieties remain tender.

SPACING: A single row will gradually exhaust subsoil moisture from an area 4 feet wide. When the seedlings are 2 to 3 inches tall, thin carefully to about 1 inch apart. When the edible part is radish size, thin to 2 inches apart and eat the thinnings, tops and all. When they've grown to golfball size, thin to 4 inches apart. When they reach the size of large lemons, thin to 1 foot apart. Given this much room and deep, open soil, the beets will continue to grow through the entire summer. Hill up some soil over the huge roots early in November to protect them from freezing.

IRRIGATION: Probably not necessary with over 4 feet of deep, open soil.

VARIETIES: I've done best with Early Wonder Tall Top; when large, it develops a thick, protective skin and retains excellent eating quality. Winterkeepers, normally sown in midsummer with irrigation, tend to bolt prematurely when sown in April.

Broccoli: *Italian Style*

Italian-style broccoli needs abundant moisture to be tender and make large flowers. Given enough elbow room, many varieties can endure long periods of moisture stress, but the smaller, woody, slow-developing florets won't be great eating. Without any irrigation, spring-sown broccoli may still be enjoyed in early summer and Purple Sprouting in March/April after overwintering.

SOWING DATE: Without any irrigation at all, mid-March through early April. With fertigation, also mid-April through mid-May. This later sowing will allow cutting throughout summer.

SPACING: Broccoli tastes better when big plants grow big, sweet heads. Allow a 4-foot-wide row. Space early sowings about 3 feet apart in the row; later sowings slated to mature during summer's heat can use 4 feet. On a fist-sized spot compacted to restore capillarity, sow a little pinch of seed atop a well- and deeply fertilized, double-dug patch of earth. Thin gradually to the best single plant by the time three or four true leaves have developed.

IRRIGATION: After mid-June, 4 to 5 gallons of drip-bucket liquid fertilizer every two to three weeks makes an enormous difference. You'll be surprised at the size of the heads and the quality of side shoots. A fertigated May sowing will be exhausted by October. Take a chance: a heavy side-dressing of strong compost or complete organic fertilizer when the rains return may trigger a massive spurt of new, larger heads from buds located below the soil's surface.

VARIETIES: Many hybrids have weak roots. I'd avoid anything that was "held up on a tall stalk" for mechanical harvest or was "compact" or that "didn't have many side-shoots." Go for larger size. Territorial's hybrid blend yields big heads for over a month, followed by abundant side shoots. Old, open-pollinated types like Italian Sprouting Calabrese, DeCicco, or Waltham 29 are highly variable, bushy, with rather coarse, large-beaded flowers, second-rate flavor, and many, many side shoots. Irrigating gardeners who can start new plants every four weeks from May through July may prefer hybrids. Dry gardeners who will want to cut side shoots for as long as possible during summer from large, well-established plants may prefer crude, open-pollinated varieties. Try both.

Broccoli: Purple Sprouting and Other Overwintering Types

SOWING DATE: It is easiest to sow in April or early May, minimally fertigate a somewhat gnarly plant through the summer, push it for size in fall and winter, and then harvest it next March. With too early a start in spring, some premature flowering may occur in autumn; still, massive blooming will resume again in spring.

Overwintering green Italian types such as ML423 (TSC) will flower in fall if sown before late June. These sorts are better started in a nursery bed around August 1 and, like overwintered cauliflower, transplanted about 2 feet apart when fall rains return, then pushed for growth with extra fertilizer in fall and winter.

SPACING: Grow like Italian-style broccoli, 3 to 4 feet apart. With nearly a whole year to grow before blooming, Purple Sprouting eventually reaches 4 to 5 feet in height and 3 to 4 feet in diameter, and yields hugely.

IRRIGATION: It is not essential to heavily fertigate Purple Sprouting, though you may G-R-O-W enormous plants for their beauty. Quality or quantity of spring harvest won't drop one bit if the plants become a little stunted and gnarly in summer, as long as you fertilize late in September to spur rapid growth during fall and winter.

Root System Vigor in the Cabbage Family

Wild cabbage is a weed and grows like one, able to successfully compete for water against grasses and other herbs. Remove all competition with a hoe, and allow this weed to totally control all the moisture and nutrients in all the earth its roots can occupy, and it grows hugely and lushly. Just for fun, I once G-R-E-W one, with tillage, hoeing, and spring fertilization but no irrigation; it ended up 5 feet tall and 6 feet in diameter.

As this highly moldable family is inbred and shaped into more and more exaggerated forms, it weakens and loses the ability to forage. Kale retains the most wild aggressiveness, Chinese cabbage perhaps the least. Here, in approximately correct order, is shown the declining root vigor and general adaptation to moisture stress of cabbage family vegetables. Each column shows the most vigorous at the top, declining as it goes down.

Adapted to dry gardening	*Not vigorous enough*
Kale	Italian broccoli, some
Purple Sprouting broccoli	varieties
Brussels sprouts, late types	Cabbage, regular market
Late savoy cabbage	types
Mid-season savoy cabbage	Brussels sprouts, early types
types	Small market-garden
Giant field-type kohlrabi	kohlrabi
Rutabaga	Cauliflower, regular "annual"
Italian broccoli (barely	Turnips and radishes
adapted)	Chinese cabbage

Brussels Sprouts

SOWING DATE: If the plants are a foot tall before the soil starts drying down, their roots will be over a foot deep; the plants will then grow hugely with a bit of fertigation. At Elkton I dry garden Brussels sprouts by sowing late April to early May. Started this soon, even late-maturing varieties may begin forming sprouts by September. Though premature bottom sprouts will "blow up" and become aphid damaged, more, higher-quality sprouts will continue to form farther up the stalk during autumn and winter.

SPACING: Grow like Italian-style broccoli, about 4 feet apart.

IRRIGATION: Without any added moisture, the plants will become stunted but will survive all summer. Side-dressing manure or fertilizer late in September (or sooner if the rains come sooner) will provoke very rapid autumn growth and a surprisingly large yield from plants that looked stressed out in August. If increasingly larger amounts of fertigation can be provided every two to three weeks, the lush Brussels sprouts plants can become 4 feet in diameter and 4 feet tall by October and yield enormously.

VARIETIES: Use late European hybrid types. At Elkton, where winters are a little milder than in the Willamette, Lunet (TSC) has the finest eating qualities. Were I farther north I'd grow hardier types like Stabolite (TSC) or Fortress (TSC). Early types are not suitable to growing with insufficient irrigation or frequent spraying to fight off aphids.

Cabbage

Forget those delicate, green supermarket cabbages unless you have unlimited amounts of water. But easiest-to-grow savoy types will do surprisingly well with surprisingly little support. Besides, savoys are the best salad material.

SOWING DATE: I suggest three sowing times: the first, a succession of early, midseason, and late savoys made in mid-March for harvest during summer; the second, late and very late varieties started late April to early May for harvest during fall and winter; the last, a nursery bed of overwintered sorts sown late in August.

SPACING: Early-maturing savoy varieties are naturally smaller and may not experience much hot weather before heading up—these may be separated by about 30 inches. The later ones are large plants and should be given 4 feet of space or 16 square feet of growing room. Sow and grow them like broccoli. Transplant overwintered cabbages from nursery beds late in October, spaced about 3 feet apart; these thrive where the squash grew.

IRRIGATION: The more fertigation you can supply, the larger and more luxuriant the plants and the bigger the heads. But even small, somewhat moisture-stressed savoys make very edible heads. In terms of increased yield for water expended, it is well worth it to provide late varieties with a few gallons of fertigation about mid-June, and a bucketful in mid-July and mid-August.

VARIETIES: Japanese hybrid savoys make tender eating but may not withstand winter. European savoys are hardier, coarser, thicker-leaved, and harder chewing. For the first sowing I suggest a succession of Japanese varieties including Salarite or Savoy Princess for earlies; Savoy Queen, King, or Savoy Ace for midsummer; and Savonarch (TSC) for late August/early September harvests. They're all great varieties. For the second sowing I grow Savonarch (TSC) for September–November cutting and a very late European hybrid type like Wivoy (TSC) for winter. Small-framed January King lacks sufficient root vigor. Springtime (TSC) and FEM218 (TSC) are the only overwintered cabbages available.

Carrots

Here's my problem. Dry-gardening carrots requires patiently waiting until the weather stabilizes before tilling and sowing. To avoid even a little bit of soil compaction, I try to sprout the seed without irrigation but always fear that hot weather will frustrate my efforts. So I till and plant too soon. And then heavy rain comes and compacts my perfectly fluffed-up soil. But the looser and finer the earth remains during their first six growing weeks, the more perfectly the roots will develop.

SOWING DATE: April at Elkton.

SPACING: Allocate 4 feet of width to a single row of carrot seed. When the seedlings are about 2 inches tall, thin to 1 inch apart. Then thin every other carrot when the roots are ⅛ to ½ inch in diameter and eat the thinnings. A few weeks later, when the carrots are about ¼ to 1 inch in diameter, make a final thinning to 1 foot apart.

IRRIGATION: Not necessary. Foliar feeding every few weeks will make much larger roots. Without any help they should grow to several pounds each.

VARIETIES: Choosing the right variety is very important. Nantes and other delicate, juicy types lack enough fiber to hold together when they get very large. These split prematurely. I've had my best results with Danvers types. I'd also try Royal Chantenay (PEA), Fakkel Mix (TSC), Stokes "Processor" types, and Topweight (ABL). Be prepared to experiment with variety. The roots will not be quite as tender as heavily watered Nantes types but are a lot better than you'd think. Huge carrots are excellent in soups and we cheerfully grate them into salads. Something about accumulating sunshine all summer makes the roots incredibly sweet.

Cauliflower

Ordinary varieties cannot forage for moisture. Worse, moisture stress at any time during the growth cycle prevents proper formation of curds. The only important cauliflowers suitable for dry gardening are overwintered types. I call them important because they're easy to grow and they'll feed the family during April and early May, when other garden fare is very scarce.

SOWING DATE: To acquire enough size to survive cold weather, overwintered cauliflower must be started on a nursery bed during the difficult heat of early August. Except south of Yoncalla, delaying sowing until September makes very small seedlings that may not be hardy enough and likely won't yield much in April unless winter is very mild, encouraging unusual growth.

SPACING: In October, transplant about 2 feet apart in rows 3 to 4 feet apart.

IRRIGATION: If you have more water available, fertilize and till up some dusty, dry soil, wet down the row, direct-seed like broccoli (but closer together), and periodically irrigate until fall. If you only moisten a narrow band of soil close to the seedlings it won't take much water. Cauliflower grows especially well in the row that held bush peas.

VARIETIES: The best are the very pricy Armado series sold by Territorial.

Chard

This vegetable is basically a beet with succulent leaves and thick stalks instead of edible, sweet roots. It is just as drought tolerant as a beet, and in dry gardening, chard is sown, spaced, and grown just like a beet. But if you want voluminous leaf production during summer, you may want to fertigate it occasionally.

VARIETIES: The red chards are not suitable for starting early in the season; they have a strong tendency to bolt prematurely if sown during that part of the year when daylength is increasing.

Corn

Broadcast complete organic fertilizer or strong compost shallowly over the corn patch in midwinter. Till as early in spring as the earth can be worked without making too many clods. Corn will germinate in pretty rough soil. High levels of nutrients in the subsoil are more important than a fine seedbed.

SOWING DATE: About the time frost danger ends. Being large seed, corn can be set deep, where soil moisture still exists even after conditions have warmed up. Germination without irrigation should be no problem.

SPACING: The farther south, the farther apart. Entirely without irrigation, I've had fine results spacing individual corn plants 3 feet apart in rows 3 feet apart, or 9 square feet per each plant. Were I around Puget Sound or in British Columbia I'd try 2 feet apart in rows 30 inches apart. Gary Nabhan describes Papago gardeners in Arizona growing individual cornstalks 10 feet apart. Grown on wide spacings, corn tends to tiller (put up multiple stalks, each stalk making one or two ears). For most urban and suburban gardeners, space is too valuable to allocate 9 square feet for producing one or at best three or four ears.

IRRIGATION: With normal sprinkler irrigation, corn may be spaced 8 inches apart in rows 30 inches apart, still yielding one or two ears per stalk.

VARIETIES: Were I a devoted sweet-corn eater without enough irrigation, I'd be buying a few dozen freshly picked ears from the back of a pickup truck parked on a corner during local harvest season. Were I a devoted corn grower without any irrigation, I'd be experimenting with various types of corn instead of sweet corn. Were I a self-sufficiency buff trying earnestly to produce all my own cereal, I'd accept that the maritime Northwest is a region where survivalists will eat wheat, rye, millet, and other small grains.

Many varieties of field corn are nearly as sweet as ordinary sweet corn, but grain varieties become starchy and tough within hours of harvest. Eaten promptly, "pig" corn is every bit as tasty as Jubilee. I've had the best dry-garden results with Northstine Dent (JSS) and Garland Flint (JSS). Hookers Sweet Indian (TSC) has a weak root system.

Cucumbers

SOWING DATE: About May 5 to 15 at Elkton.

SPACING: Most varieties usually run about 3 feet from the hill. Space the hills about 5 to 6 feet apart in all directions.

Successfully Starting Cucurbits from Seed

With cucurbits, germination depends on high-enough soil temperature and not too much moisture. Squash are the most chill and moisture tolerant, melons the least. Here's a failure-proof and simple technique that ensures you'll plant at exactly the right time.

Cucumbers, squash, and melons are traditionally sown atop a deeply dug, fertilized spot that usually looks like a little mound after it is worked and is commonly called a hill. About two weeks before the last anticipated frost date in your area, plant five or six squash seeds about 2 inches deep in a clump in the very center of that hill. Then, a week later, plant another clump at 12 o'clock. In another week, plant another clump at 3 o'clock, and continue doing this until one of the sowings sprouts. Probably the first try won't come up, but the hill will certainly germinate several clumps of seedlings. If weather conditions turn poor, a later-to-sprout group may outgrow those that came up earlier. Thin gradually to the best single plant by the time the vines are running.

When the first squash seeds appear, it is time to begin sowing cucumbers, starting a new batch each week until one emerges. When the cucumbers first germinate, it's time to try melons.

Approaching cucurbits this way ensures that you'll get the earliest possible germination while being protected against the probability that cold, damp weather will prevent germination or permanently spoil the growth prospects of the earlier seedlings.

IRRIGATION: Like melons. Regular and increasing amounts of fertigation will increase the yield several hundred percent.

VARIETIES: I've had very good results dry-gardening Amira II (TSC), even without any fertigation at all. It is a Middle Eastern–style variety that makes pickler-size, thin-skinned cukes that need no peeling and have terrific flavor. The burpless or Japanese sorts don't seem to adapt well to drought. Most slicers dry-garden excellently. Apple or Lemon are similar novelty heirlooms that make very extensive vines with aggressive roots and should be given a foot or two more elbow room. I'd avoid any variety touted as being for pot or patio, compact, or short-vined, because of a likely linkage between its vine structure and root system.

Eggplant

Grown without regular sprinkler irrigation, eggplant seems to get larger and yield sooner and more abundantly. I suspect this delicate and fairly drought-resistant tropical species does not like having its soil temperature lowered by frequent watering.

SOWING DATE: Set out transplants at the usual time, about two weeks after the tomatoes, after all frost danger has passed and after nights have stably warmed up above 50°F.

SPACING: Double dig and deeply fertilize the soil under each transplant. Separate plants by about 3 feet in rows about 4 feet apart.

IRRIGATION: Will grow and produce a few fruit without any watering, but a bucket of fertigation every three to four weeks during summer may result in the most luxurious, hugest, and heaviest-bearing eggplants you've ever grown.

VARIETIES: I've noticed no special varietal differences in ability to tolerate dryish soil. I've had good yields from regionally adapted varieties like Dusky Hybrid, Short Tom, and Early One.

Endive

A biennial member of the chicory family, endive quickly puts down a deep taproot and is naturally able to grow through prolonged drought. Because endive remains bitter until cold weather, it doesn't matter if it grows slowly through summer, just so long as rapid leaf production resumes in autumn.

SOWING DATE: On irrigated raised beds endive is sown around August 1 and heads by mid-October. The problem with dry-gardened endive is that if it is spring sown during days of increasing daylength, when germination of shallow-sown small seed is a snap, it will bolt prematurely. The crucial moment seems to be about June 1. April/May sowings bolt in July/August; after June 1, bolting won't happen until the next spring, but germination won't happen without watering. One solution is soaking the seeds overnight, rinsing them frequently until they begin to sprout, and fluid drilling them.

SPACING: The heads become huge when started in June. Sow in rows 4 feet apart and thin gradually until the rosettes are 3 inches in diameter, then thin to 18 inches apart.

IRRIGATION: Without a drop of moisture the plants, even as tiny seedlings, will grow steadily but slowly all summer, as long as no other crop is invading their root zone. The only time I had trouble was when the endive row was too close to an aggressive row of yellow crookneck squash. About August, the squash roots began occupying the endive's territory and the endive got wilty.

A light side-dressing of complete organic fertilizer or compost in late September will grow the hugest plants imaginable.

VARIETIES: Curly types seem more tolerant to rain and frost during winter than broad-leaf Batavian varieties. I prefer President (TSC).

Herbs

Most perennial and biennial herbs are actually weeds and wild hillside shrubs from Mediterranean climates similar to that of Southern California. They are adapted to growing on winter rainfall and surviving seven to nine months without rainfall every summer. In our climate, merely giving them a little more elbow room than usually offered, thorough weeding, and side-dressing the herb garden with a little compost in fall is enough coddling. Annuals such as dill and cilantro are also very drought tolerant. Basil, however, needs considerable moisture.

Kale

Depending on the garden for a significant portion of my annual caloric intake has gradually refined my eating habits. Years ago I learned to like cabbage salads as much as lettuce. Since lettuce freezes out many winters (19–21°F), this adjustment has proved very useful.

Gradually I began to appreciate kale, too, and now value it as a salad green far more than cabbage. This personal adaptation has proved very pro-survival, because even savoy cabbages do not grow as readily or yield nearly as much as kale. And kale is a tad more cold hardy than even savoy cabbage.

You may be surprised to learn that kale produces more complete protein per area occupied per time involved than any legume, including alfalfa. If it is steamed with potatoes and then mashed, the two vegetables nutritionally complement and flavor each other. Our region could probably subsist quite a bit more healthfully than at present on potatoes and kale. The key to enjoying kale as a salad component is varietal choice, preparation, and using the right parts of the plant. Read on.

SOWING DATE: With irrigation, fast-growing kale is usually started in midsummer for use in fall and winter. But kale is absolutely biennial—started in March or April, it will not bolt until the next spring. The water-wise gardener can conveniently sow kale while cool, moist soil simplifies germination. Starting this early also produces a deep root system before the soil dries much, and a much taller, very useful central stalk on *oleracea* types, while early sown Siberian (*napa*) varieties tend to form multiple rosettes by autumn, also useful at harvest time.

SPACING: Grow like broccoli, spaced 4 feet apart.

IRRIGATION: Without any water, the somewhat stunted plants will survive the summer to begin rapid growth as soon as fall rains resume. With the help of occasional fertigation they grow lushly and are enormous by September. Either way, there still will be plenty of kale during fall and winter.

HARVEST: Bundles of strong-flavored, tough, large leaves are sold in supermarkets but are the worst-eating part of the plant. If chopped finely enough, big raw leaves can be masticated and tolerated by people with good teeth. However, the tiny leaves are far tenderer and much milder. The more rosettes developed on Siberian kales, the more little leaves there are to be picked. By pinching off the central growing tip in October and then gradually stripping off the large shading leaves, *oleracea* varieties may be encouraged to put out dozens of clusters of small, succulent leaves at each leaf notch along the central stalk. The taller the stalk grown during summer, the more of these little leaves there will be. Only home gardeners can afford the time to hand pick small leaves.

VARIETIES: I somewhat prefer the flavor of Red Russian to the ubiquitous green Siberian, but Red Russian is very slightly less cold hardy. Westland Winter (TSC) and Konserva (JSS) are tall European *oleracea* varieties. Winterbor F1 (JSS, TSC) is also excellent. The dwarf "Scotch" kales, blue or green, sold by many American seed companies are less vigorous types that don't produce nearly as many gourmet little leaves. Dwarfs in any species tend to have dwarfed root systems.

Kohlrabi (Giant)

Spring-sown market kohlrabi are usually harvested before hot weather makes them get woody. Irrigation is not required if they're given a little extra elbow room. With ordinary varieties, try thinning to 5 inches apart in rows 2 to 3 feet apart and harvest by thinning alternate plants. Given this additional growing room, they may not get woody until midsummer. On my irrigated, intensive bed I always sow some more on August 1, to have tender bulbs in autumn.

Kohlrabi was once grown as a European fodder crop; slow-growing farmers' varieties grow huge like rutabagas. These field types have been crossed with table types to make "giant" table varieties that really suit dry gardening. What to do with a giant kohlrabi (or any bulb getting overblown)? Peel, grate finely, add chopped onion, dress with olive oil and black pepper, toss, and enjoy this old Eastern European mainstay.

SOWING DATE: Sow giant varieties during April, as late as possible while still getting a foot-tall plant before really hot weather.

SPACING: Thin to 3 feet apart in rows 4 feet apart.

IRRIGATION: Not absolutely necessary on deep soil, but if they get one or two thorough fertigations during summer their size may double.

VARIETIES: A few American seed companies, including Peace Seeds, have a giant kohlrabi of some sort or other. The ones I've tested tend to be woody, are crude, and throw many off-types, a high percentage of weak plants, and/or poorly shaped roots. By the time this book is in print, Territorial should list a unique Swiss variety called Superschmeltz, which is uniformly huge and stays tender into the next year.

Leeks

Unwatered spring-sown bulbing onions are impossible. Leek is the only allium I know of that may grow steadily but slowly through severe drought; the water-short gardener can depend on leeks for a fall/winter onion supply.

SOWING DATE: Start a row or several short rows about 12 inches apart on a nursery bed in March or early April at the latest. Grow thickly, irrigate during May/June, and fertilize well so the competing seedlings get leggy.

SPACING: By mid- to late June the seedlings should be slightly spindly, pencil-thick, and scallion size. With a sharp shovel, dig out the nursery row, carefully retaining 5 or 6 inches of soil below the seedlings. With a strong jet of water, blast away the soil and, while doing this, gently separate the tangled roots so that as little damage is done as possible. Make sure the roots don't dry out before transplanting. After separation, I temporarily wrap bundled seedlings in wet newspaper.

Dig out a foot-deep trench the width of an ordinary shovel and carefully place this earth next to the trench. Sprinkle in a heavy dose of organic fertilizer or strong compost, and spade that in so the soil is fluffy and fertile 2 feet down. Do not immediately refill the trench with the soil that was dug out. With a shovel handle, poke a row of 6-inch-deep holes along the bottom of the trench. If the nursery bed has grown well there should be about 4 inches of stem on each seedling before the first leaf attaches. If the weather is hot and sunny, snip off about one-third to one-half the leaf area to reduce transplanting shock. Drop one leek seedling into each hole up to the point that the first leaf attaches to the stalk, and mud it in with a cup or two of liquid fertilizer. As the leeks grow, gradually refill the trench and even hill up soil around the growing plants. This makes the better-tasting white part of the stem get as long as possible. Avoid getting soil into the center of the leek where new leaves emerge, or you'll not get them clean after harvest.

Spacing of the seedlings depends on the amount of irrigation. If absolutely none at all, set them 12 inches apart in the center of a row 4 feet wide. If unlimited water is available, give them 2 inches of separation. Or adjust spacing to the water available. The plants grow slowly through summer, but in autumn growth will accelerate, especially if they are side-dressed at this time.

VARIETIES: For dry gardening use the hardier, more vigorous winter leeks. Durabel (TSC) has an especially mild, sweet flavor. Other useful varieties include Giant Carentian (ABL), Alaska (STK), and Winter Giant (PEA).

Lettuce

Spring-sown lettuce will go to large sizes, remaining sweet and tender without irrigation if spaced 1 foot apart in a single row with 2 feet of elbow room on each side. Lettuce maturing after mid-June usually gets bitter without regular, heavy irrigation. I reserve my well-watered raised bed for this summer salad crop. Those very short of water can start fall/winter lettuce in a shaded, irrigated nursery bed mid-August through mid-September and transplant it out after the fall rains return. Here is one situation in which accelerating growth with cloches or cold frames would be very helpful.

Melons

SOWING DATE: As soon as they'll germinate outdoors—at Elkton, May 15 to June 1. Thin to a single plant per hill when there are about three true leaves and the vines are beginning to run.

SPACING: Most varieties will grow a vine reaching about 8 feet in diameter. Space the hills 8 feet apart in all directions.

IRRIGATION: Fertigation every two to three weeks will increase the yield by two or three times and may make the melons sweeter. Release the water/fertilizer mix close to the center of the vine, where the taproot can use it.

VARIETIES: Adaptation to our cool climate is critical with melons; use varieties sold by our regional seed companies. Yellow Doll watermelons (TSC) are very early and seem the most productive under the most droughty conditions. I've had reasonable results from most otherwise regionally adapted cantaloupes and muskmelons. Last year a new hybrid variety, Passport (TSC), proved several weeks earlier than I'd ever experienced and was extraordinarily prolific and tasty.

Onions/Scallions

The usual spring-sown, summer-grown bulb onions and scallions only work with abundant irrigation. But the water-short, water-wise gardener can still supply the kitchen with onions or onion substitutes year-round. Leeks take care of November through early April. Overwintered bulb onions handle the rest of the year. Scallions may also be harvested during winter.

SOWING DATE: Started too soon, overwintered or short-day bulbing onions (and sweet scallions) will bolt and form seed instead of bulbing.

Water-Wise Cucurbits

The root systems of this family are far more extensive than most people realize. Usually a taproot goes down several feet and then, soil conditions permitting, thickly occupies a large area, ultimately reaching down 5 to 8 feet. Shallow feeder roots also extend laterally as far as or farther than the vines reach at their greatest extent.

Dry gardeners can do several things to assist cucurbits. First, make sure there is absolutely no competition in their root zone. This means *one plant per hill*, with the hills separated in all directions a little farther than the greatest possible extent of the variety's ultimate growth. Common garden lore states that squashes droop their leaves in midsummer heat and that this trait cannot be avoided and does no harm. But if they're grown as described above, and on deep, open soil, capillarity and surface moisture make midday wilting unlikely, even if there is no watering. Two plants per hill do compete and make each other wilt.

Second, double dig and fertilize the entire lateral root zone. Third, as much as possible, avoid walking where the vines will ultimately reach to avoid compaction. Finally, *do not transplant them*. This breaks the taproot and makes the plant more dependent on lateral roots seeking moisture in the top 18 inches of soil.

Started too late they'll be too small and possibly not hardy enough to survive winter. About August 15 at Elkton I sow thickly in a well-watered and very fertile nursery bed. If you have more than one nursery row, separate them by about 12 inches. Those who miss this window of opportunity can start transplants in early October and cover with a cloche immediately after germination, to accelerate seedling growth during fall and early winter.

Start scallions in a nursery just like overwintered onions, but earlier so they're large enough for the table during winter; I sow them about mid-July.

SPACING: When seedlings are about pencil thick (December/January for overwintering bulb onions), transplant them about 4 or 5 inches apart in a single row with a couple of feet of elbow room on either side. I've found I get the best growth and largest bulbs if they follow potatoes. After the potatoes are dug in early October I immediately fertilize the area heavily and till, preparing the onion bed. Klamath Basin farmers usually grow a similar rotation: hay, potatoes, onions.

Transplant scallions in October with the fall rains, about 1 inch apart in rows at least 2 feet apart.

IRRIGATION: Not necessary. However, side-dressing the transplants will result in much larger bulbs or scallions. Scallions will bolt in April; the bulbers go tops-down and begin drying down as the soil naturally dries out.

VARIETIES: I prefer the sweet and tender Lisbon (TSC) for scallions. For overwintered bulb onions, grow very mild but poorly keeping Walla Walla Sweet (JSS), Buffalo (TSC), a better keeper, or whatever Territorial is selling at present.

Parsley

SOWING DATE: Plant in March. Parsley seed takes two to three weeks to germinate.

SPACING: Thin to 12 inches apart in a single row 4 feet wide. Five plants should overwhelm the average kitchen.

IRRIGATION: Not necessary unless yield falls off during summer, and that is very unlikely. Parsley's very deep, foraging root system resembles that of its relative, the carrot.

VARIETIES: If you use parsley for greens, variety is not critical, though the gourmet may note slight differences in flavor or amount of leaf curl. Another type of parsley is grown for edible roots that taste much like parsnip. These should have their soil prepared as carefully as though growing carrots.

Peas

This early crop matures without irrigation. Both pole and bush varieties are planted thickly in single rows about 4 feet apart. I always overlook some pods, which go on to form mature seed. Without overhead irrigation, this seed will sprout strongly next year. Alaska (soup) peas grow the same way.

Peppers

Pepper plants on raised beds spaced the usually recommended 16 to 24 inches apart undergo intense root competition, even before their leaves form a canopy. With or without unlimited irrigation, the plants will get much larger and bear more heavily with elbow room.

SOWING DATE: Set out transplants at the usual time. Double dig a few square feet of soil beneath each seedling, and make sure fertilizer gets incorporated all the way down to 2 feet deep.

SPACING: Three feet apart in rows 3 to 4 feet apart.

IRRIGATION: Without any irrigation only the most vigorous, small-fruited varieties will set anything. For an abundant harvest, fertigate every three or four weeks. For the biggest pepper plants you ever grew, fertigate every two weeks.

VARIETIES: The small-fruited types, both hot and sweet, have much more aggressive root systems and generally adapt better to our region's cool weather. I've had best results with Cayenne Long Slim, Gypsy, Surefire, Hot Portugal, the "cherries" both sweet and hot, Italian Sweet, and Petite Sirah.

Potatoes

Humans domesticated potatoes in the cool, arid high plateaus of the Andes, where annual rainfall averages 8 to 12 inches. The species finds our dry summer quite comfortable. Potatoes produce more calories per unit of land than any other temperate crop. Irrigated potatoes yield more calories and two to three times as much watery bulk and indigestible fiber as those grown without irrigation, but the same variety dry gardened can contain about 30 percent more protein, far more mineral nutrients, and taste better.

SOWING DATE: I make two sowings. The first is a good-luck ritual done religiously on March 17th—St. Patrick's Day. Rain or shine, in untilled mud or finely worked and deeply fluffed earth, I still plant 10 or 12 seed potatoes of an early variety. This planting provides for our summer potato needs.

The main sowing waits until frost is unlikely and I can dig the potato rows at least 12 inches deep with a spading fork, working in fertilizer as deeply as possible and ending up with a finely pulverized 24-inch-wide bed. At Elkton, this is usually mid- to late April. There is no rush to plant. Potato vines are not frost hardy. If frosted they'll regrow, but being burned back to the ground lowers the final yield.

SPACING: I presprout my seeds by spreading them out in daylight at room temperature for a few weeks, and then plant one whole, sprouting, medium-size potato every 18 inches down the center of the row. Barely cover the seed potato. At maturity there should be 2½ to 3 feet of soil unoccupied with the roots of any other crop on each side of the row. As the vines emerge, gradually scrape soil up over them with a hoe. Let the vines grow about 4 inches, then pull up about 2 inches of cover. Let another 4 inches grow, then hill up another 2 inches. Continue doing this until the vines begin blooming. At that point there should be a mound of loose, fluffy soil about 12 to 16 inches high gradually filling with tubers lushly covered with blooming vines.

IRRIGATION: Not necessary. In fact, if large water droplets compact the loose soil you scraped up, that may interfere with maximum tuber enlargement. However, after the vines are a foot long or so, foliar feeding every week or 10 days will increase the yield.

VARIETIES: The water-wise gardener's main potato problem is too-early maturity, and then premature sprouting in storage. Early varieties like Yukon Gold—even popular midseason ones like Yellow Finn—don't keep well unless they're planted late enough to brown off in late September. That's no problem if they're irrigated. But planted in late April, earlier varieties will shrivel by August. Potatoes only keep well when very cool, dark, and moist—conditions almost impossible to create on the homestead during summer. The best August compromise is to leave mature potatoes undug, but soil temperatures are in the 70s during August, and by early October, when potatoes should be lifted and put into storage, they'll already be sprouting. Sprouting in October is acceptable for the remainders of my St. Pat's Day sowing that I am keeping over for seed next spring. It is not OK for my main winter storage crop. Our climate requires very late, slow-maturing varieties that can be sown early but that don't brown off until September. Late types usually yield more, too.

Most of the seed potato varieties found in garden centers are early or midseason types chosen by farmers for yield without regard to flavor or nutrition. One, Nooksack Cascadian, is a very late variety grown commercially around Bellingham, Washington. Nooksack is pretty good if you like white, all-purpose potatoes.

There are much better home garden varieties available in Ronninger's catalog, all arranged according to maturity. For the ultimate in earlies I suggest Red Gold. For main harvests I'd try Indian Pit, Carole, German Butterball, Siberian, or a few experimental row-feet of any other late variety taking your fancy.

Rutabagas

Rutabagas have wonderfully aggressive root systems and are capable of growing continuously through long, severe drought. But where I live, the results aren't satisfactory. Here's what happens. If I start rutabagas in early April and space them about 2 to 3 feet apart in rows 4 feet apart, by October they're the size of basketballs and look pretty good; unfortunately, I harvest a hollow shell full of cabbage root maggots. Root maggots are at their peak in early June. That's why I got interested in dry-gardening giant kohlrabi.

In 1991 we had about 2 surprising inches of rain late in June, so as a test I sowed rutabagas on July 1. They germinated without more irrigation, but going into the hot summer as small plants with limited root systems and no irrigation at all they became somewhat stunted. By October 1 the tops were still small and a little gnarly; big roots had not yet formed. Then the rains came and the rutabagas began growing rapidly. By November there was a pretty nice crop of medium-size, good-eating roots.

I suspect that farther north, where evaporation is not so severe and midsummer rains are slightly more common, if a little irrigation were used to start rutabagas about July 1, a decent unwatered crop might be had most years. And I am certain that if sown at the normal time (July 15) and grown with minimal irrigation but well spaced out, they'll produce acceptably.

VARIETIES: Stokes Altasweet (STK, TSC) has the best flavor.

Sorrel

This weedlike, drought-tolerant salad green is little known and underappreciated. In summer the leaves get tough and strong flavored; if other greens are available, sorrel will probably be unpicked. That's OK. During fall, winter, and spring, sorrel's lemony taste and delicate, tender texture balance tougher savoy cabbage and kale and turn those crude vegetables into very acceptable salads. Serious salad-eating families might want the production of 5 to 10 row-feet.

SOWING DATE: The first year you grow sorrel, sow mid-March to mid-April. The tiny seed must be placed shallowly, and it sprouts much more readily when the soil stays moist. Plant a single furrow centered in a row 4 feet wide.

SPACING: As the seedlings grow, thin gradually. When the leaves are about the size of ordinary spinach, individual plants should be about 6 inches apart.

IRRIGATION: Not necessary in summer—you won't eat it anyway. If production lags in fall, winter, or spring, side-dress the sorrel patch with a little compost or organic fertilizer.

MAINTENANCE: Sorrel is perennial. If an unusually harsh winter freeze kills off the leaves, it will probably come back from root crowns in early spring. You'll welcome it after losing the rest of your winter crops. In spring of the second and succeeding years, sorrel will make seed. Seed making saps the plant's energy, and the seeds may naturalize into an unwanted weed around the garden. So, before any seed forms, cut all the leaves and seed stalks close to the ground; use the trimmings as a convenient mulch along the row. If you move the garden or want to relocate the patch, do not start sorrel again from seed. In any season dig up a few plants, divide the root masses, trim off most of the leaves to reduce transplanting shock, and transplant 1 foot apart. Occasional unique plants may be more reluctant to make seed stalks than most others. Since seed stalks produce few edible leaves and the leaves on them are very harsh flavored, making seed is an undesirable trait. So I propagate only seed-shy plants by root cuttings.

Spinach

Spring spinach is remarkably more drought tolerant than it would appear from its delicate structure and the succulence of its leaves. A bolt-resistant, long-day variety bred for summer harvest sown in late April may still yield pickable leaves in late June or even early July without any watering at all, if thinned to 12 inches apart in rows 3 feet apart.

Squash, Winter and Summer

SOWING DATE: Having warm-enough soil is everything. At Elkton I first attempt squash about April 15. In the Willamette, May 1 is usual. Farther north, squash may not come up until June 1. Dry gardeners should not transplant squash; the taproot must not be broken.

SPACING: The amount of room to give each plant depends on the potential of a specific variety's maximum root development. Most vining winter squash can completely occupy a 10-foot-diameter circle. Sprawly heirloom summer squash varieties can desiccate an 8- or 9-foot-diameter circle. Thin each hill to one plant, not two or more as is recommended in the average garden book. There must be no competition for water.

IRRIGATION: With winter storage types, an unirrigated vine may yield 15 pounds of squash after occupying a 10-foot-diameter circle for an entire growing season. However, starting about July 1, if you support that vine by supplying liquid fertilizer every two to three weeks you may harvest 60 pounds of squash from the same area. The first fertigation may only need 2 gallons. Then mid-July give 4; about August 1, 8; August 15, feed 15 gallons. After that date, solar intensity and temperatures decline, growth rate slows, and water use also decreases. On September 1 I'd add about 8 gallons and about 5 more on September 15 if it hadn't yet rained significantly. Total water: 42 gallons. Total increase in yield: 45 pounds. I'd say that's a good return on water invested.

VARIETIES: For winter squash, all the vining winter varieties in the *C. maxima* or *C. pepo* family seem acceptably adapted to dry gardening. These include Buttercup, Hubbard, Delicious, Sweet Meat, Delicata, Spaghetti, and Acorn. I wouldn't trust any of the newer compact bush winter varieties so popular on raised beds. Despite their reputation for drought tolerance, *C. mixta* varieties (or cushaw squash) were believed to be strictly hot desert or humid-tropical varieties, unable to mature in our cool climate. However, Pepita (PEA) is a *mixta* that is early enough and seems entirely unbothered by a complete lack of irrigation. The enormous vine sets numerous good keepers with mild-tasting, light yellow flesh.

Obviously, the compact bush summer squash varieties so popular these days are not good candidates for withstanding long periods without irrigation. The old heirlooms like Black Zucchini (ABL) (not Black Beauty!) and warty Yellow Crookneck grow enormous, high-yielding plants whose extent nearly rivals that of the largest winter squash. They also grow a dense leaf cover, making the fruit a little harder to find. These are the only American heirlooms still readily available. Black Zucchini has become very raggedy; anyone growing it should be prepared to plant several vines and accept that at least one-third of them will throw rather off-type fruit. It needs the work of a skilled plant breeder. Yellow Crookneck is still a fairly "clean" variety offering good uniformity. Both have more flavor and are less watery than the modern summer squash varieties. Yellow Crookneck is especially rich, probably due to its thick, oily skin; most gardeners who once grow the old Crookneck never again grow any other kind.

Both Yellow Crookneck and Black Zucchini begin yielding several weeks later than the modern hybrids. However, as the summer goes on they will produce quite a bit more squash than new hybrid types. I now grow five or six fully irrigated early hybrid plants like Seneca Zucchini too. As soon as my picking bucket is being filled with later-to-yield Crooknecks, I pull out the Senecas and use the now empty irrigated space for fall crops.

Tomatoes

With dry-gardened tomato vines, there's no point in elaborate methods such as trellising, pruning, or training. Their root systems must be allowed to control all the space they can without competition, so allow the vines to sprawl as well. And pruning the leaf area of indeterminates is counterproductive: to grow hugely, the roots need food from a full complement of leaves.

SOWING DATE: Set out transplants at the usual time. They might also be jump started under cloches two to three weeks before the last frost, to make better use of natural soil moisture.

SPACING: Depends greatly on variety. The root system can occupy as much space as the vines will cover and then some.

IRRIGATION: Especially on determinate varieties, periodic fertigation will greatly increase yield and size of fruit. The old indeterminate sprawlers will produce through an entire summer without any supplemental moisture, but yield even more in response to irrigation.

VARIETIES: With or without irrigation or anywhere in between, when growing tomatoes west of the Cascades, nothing is more important than choosing the right variety. Not only does it have to be early and able to set and ripen fruit when nights are cool, but to grow through months without watering, the plant must be highly indeterminate. This makes a built-in conflict: most of the sprawly, huge, old heirloom varieties are rather late to mature. But cherry tomatoes are always far earlier than big slicers.

If I had to choose only one variety it would be the old heirloom Red Cherry. A single plant is capable of covering a 9- to 10-foot-diameter circle if fertigated from mid-July through August. The enormous yield of a single fertigated vine is overwhelming.

Red Cherry is a little acid and tart. Non-acid, indeterminate cherry types like Sweetie, Sweet 100, and Sweet Millions are also workable but not as aggressive as Red Cherry. I wouldn't depend on most bush cherry tomato varieties. But our earliest cherry variety of all, OSU's Gold Nugget, must grow a lot more root than top, for, with or without supplemental water, Gold Nugget sets heavily and ripens enormously until mid-August, when it peters out from overbearing (not from moisture stress). Gold Nugget quits just about when the later cherry or slicing tomatoes start ripening heavily.

Other well-adapted early determinates such as Oregon Spring and Santiam may disappoint you. Unless fertigated they'll set and ripen some fruit but may become stunted in midsummer. However, a single indeterminate Fantastic Hybrid will cover a 6- to 7-foot-diameter circle, and grow and ripen tomatoes until frost with only a minimum of water. I think Stupice (ABL, TSC) and Early Cascade are also quite workable (and earlier than Fantastic in Washington).

My Own Garden Plan

CHAPTER 6

This chapter explains my own dry garden plan. An illustration of the plan appears on the last page of the color insert. Any garden plan is a product of compromises and preferences; my garden is not intended to become yours. But, all modesty aside, this plan results from 20 continuous years of serious vegetable gardening and some small degree of regional wisdom.

My wife and I are what I dub "vegetablitarians." Not vegetarians, or lacto-ovo vegetarians, because we're not ideologues and eat meat on rare, usually festive occasions in other peoples' houses. But over 80 percent of our calories are from vegetable, fruit, or cereal sources and the remaining percentage is from fats or dairy foods. The purpose of my garden is to provide at least half the actual calories we eat year-round; most of the rest comes from home-baked bread made with freshly ground whole grains. I put at least one very large bowl of salad on the table every day, winter and summer. I keep us in potatoes nine months a year and produce a year's supply of onions or leeks. To break the dietary monotony of November to April, I grow as wide an assortment of winter vegetables as possible and put most produce departments to shame from June through September, when the summer vegies are "on."

The garden may seem unusually large, but in accordance with Solomon's First Law of Abundance, there's a great deal of intentional waste. My garden produces two to three times the amount of food needed during the year so moochers, poachers, guests, adult daughters accompanied by partners, husbands, and children, mistakes, poor yields, and failures of individual vegetables are inconsequential. Besides, gardening is fun.

My garden is laid out in 125-foot-long rows and one equally long raised bed. (In the descriptions that follow and in the garden plan illustration, I've numbered the rows beginning on one side of the raised bed and moving outward, then going to the other side of the raised bed and moving outward again.) Each row grows only one or two types of vegetables. The central focus of my water-wise garden is its irrigation system. Two lines of low-angle sprinklers, only 4 feet apart, straddle an intensively irrigated raised bed running down the center of the garden. The sprinklers I use are Naans, a unique Israeli design that emits very little water and throws at a very low angle (available from TSC and some garden centers). Their maximum reach is about 18 feet; each sprinkler is about 12 feet from its neighbor. On the illustration of the garden plan, the sprinklers are indicated by a circled x. Readers unfamiliar with sprinkler system design are advised to study the irrigation chapter in Growing Vegetables West of the Cascades.

On the far left side of the garden plan illustration is a graphic representation of the uneven application of water put down by this sprinkler system. The 4-foot-wide raised bed gets lots of water, uniformly distributed. Farther away, the amount applied decreases rapidly. About half as much water lands only 6 feet from the edge of the raised bed as on the bed itself. Beyond that, the amount tapers off to insignificance. During summer's heat the farthest 6 feet is barely moistened on top, but no water effectively penetrates the dry surface. Crops are positioned according to their need for or ability to benefit from supplementation.

The Raised Bed

Crops demanding the most water are grown on the raised bed. These include a succession of lettuce plantings designed to fill the summer salad bowl, summer spinach, spring kohlrabi, my celery patch, scallions, Chinese cabbages, radishes, and various nursery beds that start overwintered crops for transplanting later. Perhaps the bed seems too large just for salad greens. But one entire meal every day consists largely of fresh, raw, high-protein green leaves; during summer, looseleaf or semi-heading lettuce is our salad item of choice. And our individual salad bowls are larger than most families of six might consider adequate to serve all of them together.

If water were severely rationed, I could irrigate the raised bed with hose and nozzle and dry garden the rest, but as it is, rows 1, 2, 7, and 8 do get significant but lesser amounts from the sprinklers. Most of the rows hold a single plant family needing similar fertilization and handling or, for convenience, that are sown at the same time.

Row 1: Succession Plantings

The row's center is about 3 feet from the edge of the raised bed. In March I sow my very first salad greens down half this row—mostly assorted leaf lettuce plus some spinach—and six closely spaced early Seneca Hybrid zucchini plants. The greens are all cut by mid-June; by mid-July my better-quality Yellow Crookneck squash come on, so I pull the zucchini. Then I till that entire row, refertilize, and sow half to rutabagas. The nursery bed of leek seedlings has gotten large enough to transplant at this time, too. These go into a trench dug into the other half of the row. The leeks and rutabagas could be reasonably productive located farther from the sprinklers, but no vegetables benefit more from abundant water or are more important to a self-sufficient kitchen. Rutabagas break the winter monotony of potatoes; leeks vitally improve winter salads, and leeky soups are a household staple from November through March.

Row 2: Semi-Drought Tolerant Brassicas

Row 2 gets about half the irrigation of row 1 and about one-third as much as the raised bed, and so is wider, to give the roots more room. One-third of the row grows savoy cabbage, the rest, Brussels sprouts. These brassicas are spaced 4 feet apart and by summer's end the lusty sprouts form a solid hedge 4 feet tall.

Row 3: Kale

Row 3 grows 125 feet of various kales sown in April. There's just enough overspray to keep the plants from getting gnarly. I prefer kale to not get very stunted, if only for aesthetics: on my soil, one vanity fertigation about mid-July keeps this row looking impressive all summer. Other gardens with poorer soil might need more support. This much kale may seem an enormous oversupply, but between salads and steaming greens with potatoes we manage to eat almost all the tender small leaves it grows during winter.

Row 4: Root Crops

Mostly carrots, a few beets. No irrigation, no fertigation, none needed. One hundred carrots weighing in at around 5 pounds each and 20-some beets of equal magnitude make our year's supply for salads, soups, and a little juicing.

Row 5: Dry-Gardened Salads

This row holds a few crowns of French sorrel, a few feet of parsley. Over a dozen giant kohlrabi are spring sown, but over half the row grows endive. I give this row absolutely no water. Again, when contemplating the amount of space it takes, keep in mind that this endive and kohlrabi must help fill our salad bowls from October through March.

Row 6: Peas, Overwintered Cauliflower, and All Solanaceae

Half the row grows early bush peas. Without overhead irrigation to bother them, unpicked pods form seed that sprouts excellently the next year. This half of the row is rotary tilled and fertilized again after the pea vines come out. Then it stays bare through July while capillarity somewhat recharges the soil. About August 1, I wet the row's surface down with hose and fan nozzle and sow overwintered cauliflower seed. To keep the cauliflower from stunting I must lightly hand sprinkle the row's center twice weekly through late September. Were water more restricted, I could start my cauliflower seedlings in a nursery bed and transplant them here in October.

The other half of the row is home to the Solanaceae: tomatoes, peppers, and eggplant. I give this row a little extra width because pea vines run, and I fertigate my Solanaceae, preferring sprawly tomato varieties that may cover an 8-foot-diameter circle. I leave a couple feet of bare earth along the outside because the neighboring grasses will deplete soil moisture along the edge of the garden.

Row 7: Water-Demanding Brassicas

Moving away from irrigation on the other side of the raised bed, I grow a succession of hybrid broccoli varieties and late fall cauliflower. The broccoli is sown several times, 20 row-feet each sowing, done about April 15, June 1, and July 15. The late cauliflower goes in about July 1. If necessary I could use much of this row for quick crops that would be harvested before I wanted to sow broccoli or cauliflower, but I don't need more room. The first sowings of broccoli are pulled out early enough to permit succession sowings of arugula or other late salad greens.

Row 8: The Trellis

Here I erect a 125-foot-long, 6-foot-tall net trellis for gourmet delicacies like pole peas and pole beans. The bean vines block almost all water that would reach beyond it and so this row gets more irrigation than it otherwise might. The peas are harvested early enough to permit a succession sowing of Purple Sprouting broccoli in mid-July. Purple Sprouting needs a bit of sprinkling to germinate in the heat of midsummer, but, being as vigorous as kale, once up, it grows adequately on the overspray from the raised bed. The beans would be overwhelmingly abundant if all were sown at one time, so I plant them in two stages about three weeks apart. Still, a great many beans go unpicked. These are allowed to form seed, are harvested before they quite dry, and crisp under cover away from the sprinklers. We get enough seed from this row for planting next year, plus all the dry beans we care to eat during winter. Dry beans are hard to digest, and as we age we eat fewer and fewer of them. In previous years I've grown entire rows of dry legume seeds at the garden's edge.

Row 9: Cucurbits

This row is so wide because here are grown all the spreading cucurbits. The pole beans in row 8 tend to prevent overspray; this dryness is especially beneficial to humidity-sensitive melons, serendipitously reducing their susceptibility to powdery mildew diseases. All cucurbits are fertigated every three weeks. The squash will have fallen apart by the end of September, melons are pulled out by mid-September. The area is then tilled and fertilized, making space to transplant overwintered spring cabbages, other overwintered brassicas, and winter scallions in October. These transplants are dug from nurseries on the irrigated raised bed. I could also set cold frames here and force tender salad greens all winter.

Row 10: Unirrigated Potatoes

This single long row satisfies a potato-loving household all winter. The quality of these dry-gardened tubers is so high that my wife complains if she must buy a few new potatoes from the supermarket after our supplies have become so sprouty and/or shriveled that they're not tasty any longer.

CHAPTER 7

A Water-Wise Back Yard

I am an unusually fortunate gardener. After seven years at Lorane, Oregon, struggling on one of the poorest growing sites in this region, we now live on 16 acres of mostly excellent, deep soil, on the floor of a beautiful, coastal Oregon valley. My house and gardens are perched safely above the 100-year flood line, there's a big, reliable well, and if I ever want more than 20 gallons per minute in midsummer, there's the virtually unlimited Umpqua River to draw from. Much like a master skeet shooter who uses a .410 to make the sport more interesting, I have chosen to dry garden.

Few are this lucky. These days the majority of North Americans live an urban struggle. Their houses are as often perched on steep, thinly soiled hills or gooey, difficult clay as on a tiny fragment of what was once prime farmland. And never does the municipal gardener have one vital liberty I do: to choose which one-sixth of an acre in his 14-acre "back yard" he'll garden on this year.

I was a suburban backyard gardener for five years before deciding to homestead. I've frequently recalled this experience while learning to dry garden. What follows in this chapter are some strategies to guide the urban in becoming more water-wise.

WATER CONSERVATION IS THE MOST IMPORTANT FIRST STEP

After it rains or after sprinkler irrigation, water evaporates from the surface until a desiccated earth mulch develops. Frequent light watering increases this type of loss. Where lettuce, radishes, and other shallow-rooting vegetables are growing, perhaps it is best to accept this loss or spread a thin mulch to reduce it. But most vegetables can feed deeper, so if wetting the surface can be avoided, a lot of water can be saved.

Even sprinkling longer and less frequently helps accomplish that. Half the reason that drip systems are more efficient is that the surface isn't dampened and virtually all water goes deep into the earth. The other half is that they avoid evaporation that occurs while water sprays through the air between the nozzle and the soil. Sprinkling at night or early in the morning, when there is little or no wind, prevents almost all of this type of loss.

To use drip irrigation it is not necessary to invest in pipes, emitters, filters, pressure regulators, and so forth. I've already explained how recycled plastic buckets or other large containers can be improvised into very effective drip emitters. Besides, drip tube systems are not trouble free: having the beds covered with fragile pipes makes hoeing dicey, while every emitter must be periodically checked against blockage.

When using any type of drip system it is especially important to relate the amount of water applied to the depth of the soil and to the crops' root development. There's no sense adding more water than the earth can hold. Calculating the optimum amount of water to apply from a drip system requires applying substantial, practical intelligence to evaluating the following factors: soil water-holding capacity and accessible depth; how deep the root systems have developed; how broadly the water spreads out below each emitter (dispersion); rate of loss due to transpiration. All but one of these factors—dispersion—are adequately discussed elsewhere in *Water-Wise Vegetables*.

A drip emitter on sandy soil moistens the earth nearly straight down with little lateral dispersion; 1 foot below the surface the wet area might only be 1 foot in diameter. Conversely, when you drip moisture into a clay soil, though the surface may seem dry, 18 inches away from the emitter and just 3 inches down the earth may become saturated with water, while a few inches deeper, significant dispersion may reach out nearly 24 inches. On sandy soil, emitters on 12-inch centers are hardly close enough together, while on clay, 30- or even 36-inch centers are sufficient.

Another important bit of data to enter into your arithmetic: 1 cubic foot of water equals about 5 gallons. A 12-inch-diameter circle equals 0.75 square feet ($a = \pi r^2$), so 1 cubic foot of water (5 gallons) dispersed from a single emitter will add roughly 16 inches of moisture to sandy soil, greatly overwatering a medium that can hold only an inch or so of available water per foot. On heavy clay, a single emitter may wet a 4-foot-diameter circle; on loams, 5 gallons will cover a 4-foot-diameter circle about 1 inch deep. So on deep, clay soil, 10 or even 15 gallons per application may be in order. What is the texture of your soil, its water-holding capacity, and the dispersion of a drip into it? Probably, it is somewhere in between sand and clay.

I can't specify what is optimum in any particular situation. Each gardener must consider his own unique factors and make his own estimation. All I can do is stress again that the essence of water-wise gardening is water conservation.

OPTIMIZING SPACE: PLANNING THE WATER-WISE BACKYARD GARDEN

Intensive gardening is a strategy holding that yield per square foot is the supreme goal; it succeeds by optimizing as many growth factors as possible. So a raised bed is loosened very deeply without concern for the amount of labor, while fertility and moisture are supplied virtually without limit. Intensive gardening makes sense when land is very costly and the worth of the food grown is judged against organic produce at retail—and when water and nutrients are inexpensive and/or available in unlimited amounts.

When water use is reduced, yield inevitably drops proportionately. The backyard water-wise gardener, then, must logically ask which vegetable species will give him enough food or more economic value with limited space and water. Taking maritime Northwest rainfall patterns into consideration, here's my best estimation:

Water-Wise Efficiency of Vegetable Crops
(in terms of backyard usage of space and moisture)

Efficient enough

Early spring-sown crops: peas, broccoli, lettuce, radishes, savoy cabbage, kohlrabi
Endive
Garden sorrel
Giant kohlrabi
Heirloom summer squash
Herbs: marjoram, thyme, dill, cilantro, fennel, oregano

Indeterminate tomatoes
Kale
Overwintered: onions, broccoli, cauliflower, cabbage, fava beans
Parsley, leaf and root
Pole beans
Root crops: carrots, beets, parsnips

Water-Wise Efficiency of Vegetable Crops (*continued*)

Marginal

Brussels sprouts, late

Determinate tomatoes

Eggplant

Leeks

Peppers, small fruited

Potatoes

Rutabagas

Savoy cabbage, late

Winter squash

Inefficient

Beans, bush snap

Broccoli, summer

Cauliflower

Celery

Lettuce

Peppers, bell

Radishes

Scallions, bulb onions

Sweet corn

Turnips

Have fun planning your own water-wise garden!

More Reading

About the Interlibrary Loan Service

Agricultural books, especially older ones, are not usually available at local libraries. But most municipal libraries and all universities offer access to an on-line database listing the holdings of other cooperating libraries throughout the United States. Almost any book published in this century will be promptly mailed to the requesting library. Anyone who is serious about learning by reading should discover how easy and inexpensive (or free) it is to use the Interlibrary Loan Service.

Carter, Vernon Gill, and Tom Dale. TOPSOIL AND CIVILIZATION. Norman, Okla.: University of Oklahoma Press, 1974. *The history of civilization's destruction of one ecosystem after another by plowing and deforestation, and its grave implications for our country's long-term survival.*

Cleveland, David A., and Daniela Soleri. FOOD FROM DRYLAND GARDENS: AN ECOLOGICAL, NUTRITIONAL AND SOCIAL APPROACH TO SMALL-SCALE HOUSEHOLD FOOD PRODUCTION. Tucson: Center for People, Food and Environment, 1991. *World-conscious survey of low-tech food production in semiarid regions.*

Faulkner, Edward H. PLOWMAN'S FOLLY. Norman, Okla.: University of Oklahoma Press, 1943. *This book created quite a controversy in the 1940s. Faulkner stresses the vital importance of capillarity. He explains how conventional plowing stops this moisture flow.*

Foth, Henry D. FUNDAMENTALS OF SOIL SCIENCE. Eighth Edition. New York: John Wylie & Sons, 1990. *A thorough yet readable basic soil science text at a level comfortable for university non-science majors.*

Hamaker, John D. THE SURVIVAL OF CIVILIZATION. Annotated by Donald A. Weaver. Michigan/California: Hamaker-Weaver Publishers, 1982. *Hamaker contradicts our current preoccupation with global warming*

and makes a believable case that a new epoch of planetary glaciation is com-
ing, caused by an increase in greenhouse gases. The book is also a guide to
soil enrichment with rock powders.

Kourik, Robert. DRIP IRRIGATION FOR EVERY LANDSCAPE AND ALL
CLIMATES. Santa Rosa, California: Metamorphic Press, 1992. *A thor-*
ough manual of deep irrigation, full of technical and design information.

Nabhan, Gary. THE DESERT SMELLS LIKE RAIN: A NATURALIST IN
PAPAGO INDIAN COUNTRY. San Francisco: North Point Press, 1987.
Describes regionally useful Native American dry-gardening techniques.

Russell, Sir E. John. SOIL CONDITIONS AND PLANT GROWTH. Eighth
Edition. New York: Longmans, Green & Co., 1950. *Probably the finest,*
most human soil science text ever written. Russell avoids unnecessary math-
ematics and obscure terminology. I do not recommend the recent in-print
edition, revised and enlarged by a committee.

Smith, J. Russell. TREE CROPS: A PERMANENT AGRICULTURE. New York:
Harcourt, Brace and Company, 1929. *Smith's visionary solution to upland*
erosion is growing unirrigated tree crops that produce cereal-like foods and
nuts. Should sit on the "family bible shelf" of every permaculturalist.

Solomon, Steve J. GROWING VEGETABLES WEST OF THE CASCADES.
Seattle: Sasquatch Books, 1989. *The complete regional gardening text-*
book.

_____. BACKYARD COMPOSTING. Portland, Ore.: George
van Patten Publishing, 1992. *Especially useful for its unique discussion of*
the overuse of compost and a nonideological approach to raising the most
nutritious food possible.

Stout, Ruth. GARDENING WITHOUT WORK FOR THE AGING, THE BUSY
AND THE INDOLENT. Old Greenwich, Conn.: Devin-Adair, 1961. *Stout*
presents the original thesis of permanent mulching.

Turner, Frank Newman. FERTILITY, PASTURES AND COVER CROPS
BASED ON NATURE'S OWN BALANCED ORGANIC PASTURE FEEDS.

San Diego: Rateaver, 1975. Reprinted from the 1955 Faber and Faber edition. *Organic farming using long rotations, including deeply rooted green manures developed to a high art. Turner maintained a productive organic dairy farm using subsoiling and long rotations involving tilled crops and semi-permanent grass/herb mixtures.*

van der Leeden, Frits, Fred L. Troise, and David K. Todd. THE WATER ENCYCLOPEDIA, Second Edition. Chelsea, Mich.: Lewis Publishers, 1990. *Reference data concerning every possible aspect of water.*

Weaver, John E., and William E. Bruner. ROOT DEVELOPMENT OF VEGETABLE CROPS. New York: McGraw-Hill, 1927. *Contains very interesting drawings showing the amazing depth and extent that vegetable roots are capable of in favorable soil.*

Widtsoe, John A. DRY FARMING: A SYSTEM OF AGRICULTURE FOR COUNTRIES UNDER LOW RAINFALL. New York: The Macmillan Company, 1920. *The best single review ever made of the possibilities of dry farming and dry gardening, sagely discussing the scientific basis behind the techniques. The quality of Widtsoe's understanding proves that newer is not necessarily better.*

Index

(Page numbers in bold type indicate material found in tables and illustrations.)

Special Offer:
Get Growing!

Sasquatch Books has arranged with Territorial Seed Company of Cottage Grove, Oregon, to provide you with a sample packet of seed for your Northwest water-wise garden.

Choose one of the two vegetables listed below, then fill out and send the form at the bottom of the page. Your sample seeds will be sent with a full catalog from Territorial Seed Company, offering dozens of vegetable varieties ideally suited for home gardens west of the Cascades.

Summer Squash—Yellow Crookneck (*C. pepo*)
This old-time variety may not win any beauty contests, but the flavor is unbeatable. The large, bushy plant is a heavy yielder of bright yellow, slightly warted, crookneck fruit. Good drought tolerance. 65 days to maturity.

Cherry Tomato—Red Cherry
In a good summer, these bright-red, 3/4- to 1-inch cherries will ripen around August 10. The fruit is firm, smooth, sweet and juicy, and doesn't crack. The large, indeterminate vines require no staking and bear in clusters all summer. 75–80 days to maturity.

- -

Order Form

☐ Please send me a sample packet of:

_____

(choose one of the vegetables listed above)

Name _____

Address _____

City/State/Zip _____

☐ Please send me a complete Territorial Seed Company catalog

☐ Please send me a complete Sasquatch Books catalog

Return this coupon to:

Territorial Seed Company
P.O. Box 157, Cottage Grove, OR 97424